D0668967

Haunted Encounters

Real-Life Stories of
Supernatural Experiences

Haunted Encounters

Real-Life Stories of Supernatural Experiences

Edited by Ginnie Siena Bivona, Dorothy
McConachie and Mitchel Whitington

Atriad Press • Dallas, Texas

Copyright © 2003 by Ginnie Siena Bivona,
Dorothy McConachie & Mitchel Whitington

Editors

No part of this book may be reproduced or utilized in any form or by any means,
electronic, or mechanical, including photocopying, recording or by any information storage and retrieval system without permission in writing.

Inquiries should be addressed to

Atriad Press
P.O. Box 600745
Dallas, TX 75360-0745
972-671-0002
AtriadPress.com

First Printing April 2003

Library of Congress Control Number 2003104850

International Standard Book Number 0-9740394-0-3

The editors wish to thank Alan McCuller for the outstanding cover art,
and Martha McCuller for the beautiful interior design.
We are very grateful for their contributions.

All the events, persons, locations and organizations portrayed in this book are
based on true personal accounts experienced by the authors. Any resemblance
to any other experience is unintended and entirely coincidental.

Printed in the United States of America

Introduction

The *Haunted USA* series I created with my late co-author Beth Scott very nearly didn't get beyond the talking stage. The quandary we faced over twenty-five years ago is one of the reasons I like *Haunted Encounters*.

Allow me to explain.

Though the series now numbers five titles and counting (I'm at work as sole author of the forthcoming *Haunted Homesteads*), I had to talk Beth into the project. Now you must understand that Beth had been a full-time, professional writer for nearly thirty years before we teamed up in the late 1970s. I was a relatively young college teacher/journalist who admired her ability to have forged a living from magazine and newspaper journalism for so many years. But that was the rub.

I wanted to write a book and thought she'd be a terrific collaborator. She thought I was a fine enough young man, but she didn't want any part of writing a book. So when I broached the idea of working together on such a project, she demurred.

In the world of writers, she patiently explained, there were sprinters and there were milers. Sprinters were those who preferred their assignments be wrapped up in a few hundred or a few thousand words. Poetry. Magazine articles. Newspaper features. That sort of thing. Milers wrote books. She, she said, had enjoyed being a sprinter all her life, was quite comfortable with the success she'd enjoyed, and really couldn't fathom the endurance needed to write a book.

I would not take no for an answer.

"What if we wrote a book filled with sprints?" I slyly replied. "Before you know it we'd have enough material for a book."

She couldn't argue with my logic — or at least I don't remember that she did — and we set out on our collaboration which eventually came to include *Haunted Wisconsin, Haunted Heartland, Haunted America* and, most recently, *Haunted Heritage.*

Sadly, Beth passed away in 1994, shortly before the publication of Haunted America. I've completed the last titles on my own, though we continued to share a byline.

Now, what has that got to do with the book you hold in your hands? Simply this — these gripping, firsthand stories of the supernatural are championship sprints. You can read them quickly, before the sun sets, or more slowly, savoring each delicious chill.

There is much to recommend *Haunted Encounters.*

As a long-time professor, I am partial to campus ghost stories and indeed include quite a few in my books. So I really liked "The Ghost of Winthrop Hall," written by a former editor of the campus newspaper at Endicott College in Massachusetts. Since I teach journalism, and was a college newspaper editor myself, I know the desultory affects of late night work getting the paper out, but this story transcends any hint of too much caffeine. Ms. Cook retells this spooky tale in a clear and convincing way.

You'll find ghosts and hauntings from all over the United States, and even a few wandering spirits from other nations. And for us animal lovers, "One Last Good-Bye," by Diane Kolb, makes us know more than ever that when beloved pets pass away, more than their memories remain.

I commend *Haunted Encounters* to everyone comfortable in the knowledge that our world may be populated by far more than meets the eye. Perhaps you'll be fortunate enough to meet one of those inhabitants and share your "haunted encounter" in future editions.

Michael Norman

Michael Norman is an internationally recognized writer on the paranormal. His books are available in bookstores as well as on line.

Dedication

Where does it start, a book? First in the minds of those lucky few who have learned to take their thoughts out through their fingertips and from there into *your* mind. And although you may never meet, something magical happens. There is a connection between the two of you that cannot be made in any other way.

First then, we thank our writers...the Alpha and the Omega of every book. They all use many of the same words; threads of communication, but each woven so cunningly, so cleverly, that the tapestry of every story is an amazing work of art unlike any of the others. What a glorious gift they favor us with!

But turning the writer's words into the object you hold now in your hands, ah...that's also part of the story. Editor Beth Kohler reads the manuscripts with the eye of a plastic surgeon. Nipping and tucking, tweaking and adjusting each and every word, every comma, every nuance of every sentence so that it will be just as it should be.

To Faye Voorhis, who has an eagle eye for typos. She wins the Editors *Red Pencil Award* for her painstaking perusal of every single word on every single page, and making some great catches.

A book that is pleasing to the eye reads better. Martha McCuller believes that with a passion. Every book has its own personality, and Martha delights in discovering that personality and giving it a face. Her artistic interior graphics add to the pleasure of reading.

The truth is, a book *is* judged by its cover. With about a billion books vying for your attention on the shelf, the cover is *critical*. Alan McCuller knows exactly how to create brilliant cover art that no human eye can pass over. You look. A second look. Reach out and pick it up. It can't be helped. Alan's art does that to you.

But there are others, too, we are indebted to. The kind-hearted people who graciously reviewed and commented on our book for the back cover, Kriss Stephens, Jim Fassbinder, Chris and Ginger Pennell, Steve Thrash, and Troy Taylor. And to Michael Norman, for taking time out of a very full schedule to write the introduction for an unknown face in the crowd.

And especially, *most* especially to the talented Tami Whitington. She may not have planned on being on the team, but she is. First string all the way. Suit up, Tami, you're playing.

We would be remiss if we did not recognize those who were not here, not seen, not heard...and yet, without them there is no story...the spirits, ghosts, entities, call them what you will...that make this read worthwhile.

And lastly, we thank each other for being in the right place at the right time, and having the good fortune to know what we needed to do!

Ginnie Siena Bivona, Dorothy McConachie, Mitchel Whitington
The Editors

Contents

Contents

Contents

The Wanderer

Cassandra A. Dunn

On a windy night, far from the city I had always lived in, I slept in a guest room in my mother's new house. It was two or three in the morning when I suddenly awoke with a jolt, as if shaken by someone. I glanced around the room, disoriented, trying to blink my eyes into focus, straining to identify the strange surroundings. Above my bed was a curtainless window; outside was an electric, moonless night, full of stars, devoid of the city light I was accustomed to. There were boxes of books piled high on one side of my bed. The familiarity of the boxes I had been unpacking all day brought the entire room into view with a clarity that should have calmed my nerves, but did not. The wind outside whistled persistently against the screen. What a strange feeling, to be startled awake by a house you do not know, cannot place. But there was another strange feeling there, too. A feeling that someone was in the room with me.

My attention was drawn to a soft orange glow in the corner of the room, a misty ball of light a few feet off the floor beside the bedroom door. The longer I looked at it, the more defined the light became. It expanded and elongated until a tall, narrow cloud of light hovered just above the carpet. It cast no light on the walls around it and made no shadow beneath it. Thinking it must have been a flash of lightning that had awakened me and

1

had burned the form into my retinas, I glanced around other parts of the room, expecting to see the glow follow a step ahead of my gaze. It didn't. I looked back to the orange form, now taking clear shape as a human figure. The height and broad shoulders suggested a male form, and the possibility that I was alone with a strange man in my room made me hold my breath and watch with rapt attention. Noticing the figure startled me, but I did not become truly terrified until he turned and began moving across the floor. His head, neck, and shoulders, although fuzzy around the edges, were distinct against the shadowy background. His arms and legs were not so clear, blending into the fiery mist. He did not walk across the floor with obvious steps; he simply drifted from one side of the room to the other, past the foot of my bed. He faced forward the entire time, never looking my way. It took only a few seconds for him to reach the half-closed bathroom door, and when he did, he drifted effortlessly through it and was gone. No reflection was cast in the bathroom mirror, no glow was left in the room. As suddenly as he had appeared, he was gone.

I lay perfectly still in the sudden blackness, my heart pounding with fear even as I began to rationalize all of the different things it could have been: lightning, the start of a migraine, a detaching retina, or purely a figment of my imagination. I didn't consider then that it might have been a ghost, didn't want to admit it could have been, or deal with the nagging feeling that during the time it was visible I had actually felt the presence of another being. I told myself *I must be dreaming.*

The bedroom door rattled and I leaped out of bed, glancing around for another figure. Our dog, Sara, whined in the hallway and scratched against the door again. I let her in and carried her to the bed, thankful for the company. She preferred to sleep under the covers at the foot of the bed, so I carefully tucked her in down by my knees. She growled once, then crawled out and sat upright at the foot of the bed, staring intently at the bathroom door. This dog had never been through an earthquake without behaving strangely for the entire preceding day. She had always known when something was wrong well before any of us did, and I trusted her judgment. Her reaction scared me even more, so I tried to get her to lie down, but she would not. I picked her up and tried tucking her in again, but she climbed back out and resumed her post at the foot of the bed. I lay awake for another thirty or forty minutes, watching her watch the door. The longer I lay there, the less I felt the disturbance of my glowing intruder. The fear began to drift in and out of waves of sleep. I'd doze, then awaken to see Sara still sitting at my feet and no figure present, and doze again. When I last looked at her before falling back asleep, she was still keeping watch. When daylight came, she whined to be let out of the room. Seeing that she had stayed with me all night, a rare occurrence, assured me that the event had not been a dream and left me to wonder about what had happened.

I was eighteen when I saw that ghost, visiting from college for the summer. I didn't necessarily believe in ghosts when I went to bed that night, but moments after waking, I had an undeniable sense of what I had witnessed. I found my mother preparing breakfast. I sat at the kitchen table and looked up at her, not sure how to broach the subject.

"Morning, honey. How'd you sleep?"

"Not so good," I answered, prompting her for more questions.

"I'm sorry. I know it's hard to get used to sleeping in a new place. What do you want for breakfast?"

Disappointed with her lack of interest, I decided to try another approach.

"What do you know about the people who lived here before us?"

"Not much. He was an architect and designed the house himself. He said the commute to work got to be too long for him, and after they had a baby they decided they wanted to live closer to town."

"So it was a husband, a wife, and a baby?"

"No, he had a 19-year-old son from a previous marriage. Your room was his." The casual statement gave me a chill.

"Is he still alive?"

"The architect?"

"The son."

She gave me a quizzical look. "I don't know. He was in the military. Headed for Desert Storm. French toast okay?"

I nodded. "Was the son tall and thin, with broad shoulders?"

"I don't know. I didn't meet him." She started sounding irritated with the questions.

After Mom finished making breakfast and joined me at the table, I decided to tell her what was on my mind.

"I saw a ghost in my room last night," I said matter-of-factly, looking at her face for signs of shock or horror. She remained calm, almost disinterested.

"Let me guess," she said, her voice already sarcastic. "The boy who used to live in your room?"

"I don't know who it was. I'm serious, though. Sara saw him, too." I searched her face for signs of belief. She just sat, fork halfway to her mouth, as if waiting for the punch line.

"I'm serious," I persisted. "It scared the crap out of me. He was right at the foot of my bed and he passed through the bathroom door and disappeared, then Sara came in to protect me."

"How'd Sara see the ghost if she didn't come in until after he'd gone to the bathroom?" she wanted to know.

"Maybe she saw him in the hallway," I rationalized. "Even if she didn't see him, she knew he was there. She growled at the bathroom door."

"Probably because you were staring at it and you were scaring her," she offered.

"No, I was looking at her when she growled."

Mom paused, looking at me, as if unsure of how to react.

"You have your father's sense of humor."

"But I'm not joking!" I yelled at her.

She resumed eating, the conversation over.

"Forget it. Never mind. You never listen to me anyway." I got up and started clearing breakfast dishes. Mom, seeing I was not merely acting upset for emphasis, reached over and put her hand on the small of my back.

"Honey, if you say you saw a ghost, then I believe you think you did, okay?" Her condescension was not comforting.

I shook my head and threw up my hands in surrender. "No, that doesn't help at all. I saw it, Mom. I know you don't believe me, but I swear I did. There was something in that room with me last night."

She smiled and nodded in mock acceptance and I left the room consumed by frustration.

I spent the next few weeks visiting libraries and bookstores, looking for any reference to some natural phenomena that could have caused the glowing figure to appear, but could find no other explanation. One book suggested ball lightning. I researched it just far enough to find out that its heat would've caused the wooden bathroom door to burst into flame by passing through it. Up until that point, ball lighting had been the best explanation.

At that point, I started looking up accounts of ghost appearances. I found so many stories similar to mine that I began to accept the possibility that Mom's house was haunted. I gathered from my research that I probably didn't know the ghost, or his face would've been visible to me. The fact that he had ignored me implied that either he had a clear mission in mind that did not require human help, or that he had only recently died, couldn't have seen me, and didn't know he was a ghost. I became fascinated with tales of ghost sightings, of urgent messages being conveyed through ghosts, of tragic deaths that left ghosts trapped in their childhood homes, of spirits that were hundreds of years old who chose to share their wisdom with those who dared to believe. My research finally convinced me it had indeed been a ghost, and no amount of ridicule (and I suffered a lot of it when I repeated my story back at college) was able to make me reconsider what I had seen.

Years later my stepfather, Allen, casually mentioned a "glowing thing" he'd recently seen outside of the room I'd been sleeping in that night. He mentioned it over Thanksgiving dinner, commenting to my mother that it was proof of his failing eyesight. He suspected a detaching retina.

"It was a ghost," I told him incredulously. "Mom, don't you remember?"

"Remember what?"

"I saw a ghost in that room. An orange glow in the middle of the night once."

"You did? What time did you see it?" Allen asked.

"I don't know. Probably two A.M."

"That's about the same time I saw it. Both times," he said.

"You saw it twice? Mom, why didn't you tell him about the ghost I saw?"

I recounted my experience for the family. My mother still acted as if I wasn't completely serious, half-listening as she served the meal. Everyone else was caught between wanting to believe and not wanting Mom's house to be haunted. But at least Allen believed my ghost story, and even sounded relieved to hear it, for the ghost theory meant his eyesight wasn't going after all.

We never found out what happened to the soldier who'd once lived in that bedroom, or if there had been any other deaths on the property. We speculated it could be a miner who died during the gold rush that swept over those hills. But several houseguests have seen the ghost. Always about 2 A.M., a quiet ball of light that spreads and travels, but never interacts with us, and never shares his secrets.

Cassandra Dunn was born in Berkeley, California, and grew up in the San Francisco Bay Area. She began writing when she was eight years old, authoring a fiction piece about a haunted house. She received her BA in Creative Writing from UC-San Diego, and her MFA in Creative Writing from Mills College in Oakland. She currently works as a senior editor in Berkeley. Among her writing achievements are winning the Fabili/Hoffer essay contest and the TooWrite.com writing competition. Cassandra recently completed her first book, a memoir titled *Breathing Room*, and has also completed two feature-length screenplays. Her mother continues to live in the house with the ghost. Several guests have seen him wandering along his nightly path over the years, but her mother still has never seen him.

Irrepressible Memory

Lisa Casey Perry

But each day brings its petty dust Our
soon-chok'd souls to fill, And we forget
because we must, And not because we will.
— Matthew Arnold

I t is often said that we remember what we want to remember, perhaps even embellishing our recollections with lovelier hues of color, more animated snippets of witty conversation, and generous motivations, and we forget, as a defense against losing a grip on all we know to be real and true in a world of physical laws, those experiences that terrify.

It was 1967 and I was nine. The daughter of divorced parents, I was on an extended summer visit with my father in the piney woods of East Texas. He was a schoolteacher and for a time taught English in the mystically named town of Karnack. Karnack is nestled between Uncertain, Texas, and the hauntingly beautiful Caddo Lake. All three together form a rather enchanted triangulation of geography that is rich in mysterious folklore and known for strange and ghostly sightings.

My father's brother and mother were managing a hotel in the area known as The Flying Fish Lodge, famous for having provided rooms for the cast and crew of *Creature from the Black Lagoon*, the B-movie classic of the fifties. Caddo Lake's stately cypress trees, primeval and hung like death shrouds with Spanish moss, had been the ideal setting for the dark, lovelorn swamp monster. During its heyday, the Prohibition years, the lodge had witnessed many surreptitious and covert activities, supported by a small airstrip, perhaps only 200 yards long, in front of the hotel. Luxurious, raucous parties for bootleggers and wealthy visitors were often hosted in the second-floor ballroom where guests not only illegally imbibed but gambled to their heart's content, safely hidden in the remote nowhere of a tiny corner of northeastern Texas.

By the time I came to visit the lodge, its asphalt airstrip, long since abandoned, was split up and decaying, the fertile field grasses breaking through the surface and reclaiming the petroleum amalgam as their own. I had made friends with two sisters who were a few years older than me. They were students of my father's and both had crushes on the handsome, young English teacher who looked like Elvis, which explained why the older girls were wasting their time playing Barbies and riding horses with me. The younger of the two, Becky, was particularly fond of riding and she and I spent many blissful summer days racing our horses and playing "rodeo" on the old airstrip in front of the lodge.

That summer, we had another companion, a little girl of seven or eight whose family were summer guests at the hotel. "Pammy" was tiny and slight and wore a pixie haircut like mine. She understood less about rural lake life and boy-crazy cowgirls than I did, but we all whiled away the hot, summer days together, listening to records, playing house in the hotel's vacant rooms, and holding séances in the large, empty ballroom.

Upon entering the lodge through the main front doors, the wide staircase leading to the ballroom was visible on the right. At the top of the stairway was a black wrought-iron landing, where a body might look down on those entering the main doors and raise a glass, waving a beckoning hand to come join the party. But there were no longer parties and poker games to tempt patrons of the lodge. The whole establishment had fallen into a type of budget motel kind of interest and only the first-floor rooms, the kitchen, and restaurant remained in business. My Dad and I had adjoining suites for our summer visit.

Grandmother allowed us girls to play in the empty ballroom only after much pleading on my part. The carpet was red as claret and the long room had a window wall at one end where the parking lot and airstrip could be seen. At the other end of the dance hall was a padded door, glittery and gaudy-red, leading into a small, non-functioning pantry and service area. In its former glory, the pantry would have known the bustle of tuxedoed wait staff and the occasional invasion of a champagne-giggly flapper ducking in, mistaking it for a powder room. But now it was obsolete, dank, and unlit. The old wooden counters were sagging, layered in dirt, the large wall sink barely held on to its place against the broken pipes, and only the faintest light coming through a large hole in the wall entered the room. It was the dumbwaiter, with broken cables and of no use to anyone but the mice and spiders who lived there, its lower end disappearing into the kitchen below, hidden behind utility shelves stacked with restaurant-size cans of corn and beans and ketchup.

There were no working lights in the main room, but the window wall provided plenty of light, and as one long wall was mirrored above the paneled wainscoting, the light reflected easily all around. For our conjuring, we would sit on the carpet near the end of the room, just a few feet from the pantry door, where it was somewhat darker and the flickering candlelight showed more clearly.

"And bring the Ouija board over, too," I said to Becky on the phone as we made plans for the day.

"Is Pammy going to be there? Because if she is, we'll never get a good séance going. She's too much of a scaredy-cat!"

"I don't know. I haven't seen her today yet."

"Well, Melissa isn't coming. She's grounded for staying out past curfew. Haw-haw! She's out of commission for two weeks, phone privileges, too."

"She thinks séances are dumb anyway. Hurry up. I'll wait for you out front."

I hung up the phone and went to the hotel dresser that was mine for the duration of my vacation. I had stashed two dinner candles with star-shaped glass holders, swiped from the kitchen, just for the purpose of creating our "séance mood." We had been "divining" all summer long, sometimes at Becky's house, in her bedroom, when I stayed the night, but most recently in the ballroom where we were having much better luck at "attracting the spirits."

Becky lived less than a mile away and would be walking to the lodge, with Ouija board and Barbie dolls in tow. I ran outside and waited for her on a bench outside the lodge's entrance. The morning was overcast. An approaching thunderstorm sent roiling, charcoal clouds across what would have been a blistering yellow hot sky. No reason to worry, though. Texas summertime storms sometimes came fiercely without warning and sometimes not at all, merely huffing and bluffing their way through the atmosphere.

As Becky came into view, making her way across the airstrip, Pammy joined me on the bench.

"Hey, what's up?" she asked.

"Becky's coming. See?" I pointed across the field. "We're going to have a séance in the ballroom again today. Do you want to?"

"Yeah, sure," she said unconvincingly and offered me a piece of gum.

As soon as Becky reached the two of us, she rolled her eyes and shot me the look that said she was supremely disappointed that Pammy was participating. I ignored it.

We pounded our way up the stairs and opened the door to the big room.

"Ooooh. It's dark in here today," Pammy whined.

"That's just 'cause the sun's behind the clouds. We've got candles. It'll be cool!" Becky unloaded her armful of stuff in the middle of the floor and then pulled some paper matches from her jeans pocket. Leaving the dolls in a heap, the three of us retreated to the far darkened corner of the room and sat down, placing the Ouija board in the center of our little spiritual assembly. We lit the two candles and placed them well outside our circle, where we wouldn't knock them over.

"Okay, y'all. No laughing this time," Becky started to lecture. "If we're gonna play, then we'll play, but if we're gonna call up the dead, then we need to con-cen-trate!" She said the last word slowly, each syllable sounding as though it were meant to hypnotize.

13

After some disagreement over whom we would summon — dead relatives were out, Pammy didn't know who James Dean was, and I didn't want to bother Shakespeare — it was decided we would simply ask if any spirits were available to us.

Giggling, false starts out of the way, the three of us planted our fingertips on the planchette, or the "pointer" as we called it, and closed our eyes.

"Con-cen-trate," Becky lulled, then began her plea to the other side. "Spirits of the other world, we would like to speak with you. Are there any spirits here in this room who will communicate?" The planchette was motionless. I could hear Pammy breathing shallowly.

"Spirits of The Flying Fish Lodge, we implore you to speak with us! Are you here?" The planchette began to move, ever so slowly. I thought I felt Becky pushing a little and was annoyed. We each opened our eyes a little to watch as the planchette rested on the board's affirmative answer, YES.

"Do you have a message for us?" Becky asked.

Immediately, the little planchette began moving again.

"L," Pammy whispered. She chewed her gum deliberately.

"E. Becky, are you moving the pointer?"

"No. Hush. I'm not doing anything."

"A."

"Leann? Learn? What?" I felt a lump turn over in my stomach.

"V."

"Leave! It's telling us to leave!" Becky shouted. Pammy screamed and we all broke loose from the planchette. Pammy jumped to her feet and started screaming again I leaped up to calm her down and as I did I saw movement in the mirror, slowly, darkly, like crawling shadows, all over the mirrored wall, and then the shadows were spinning, twirling into almost recognizable...wait...were they dancing?

That's when I closed my eyes and started screaming in unison with Pammy. Terrified, Becky yelled at us both to shut up and calm down. We couldn't. I couldn't. I had seen them! In my panic, clutching Pammy, I tried to exit the room, but we opened the pantry door instead of the proper exit. The pitch-black pantry intensified our hysteria. Becky ran in after us crying.

"Come on!" she yelled. "Let's get out of here!" She grabbed my hand and I held Pammy's as we felt our way along the wooden counters and out of the pantry. Suddenly, a sound like a low, deep mechanical roar started from somewhere far away and then began filling the room like a train getting closer.

"It's the dumbwaiter!" Becky screamed.

I don't remember much after that. I know that after my dad calmed me down, we were forbidden to play upstairs. "That hole in the wall is too dangerous for y'all to be up there." He retrieved the board and Becky's Barbies. I got in trouble for taking candles and matches upstairs. Pammy's parents were furious and wouldn't allow her to play with us anymore.

Terrifying as the event had been, I nevertheless managed to file it away somewhere in the recesses of my mind, and though plagued by nightmares and "creepy feelings" I eventually forgot why I had been so afraid. The remembering of it came lurking back as unexplainably as the forgetting, perhaps entreating my adult rationale to reexamine the event and name the ghosts as clouds or childish hysteria, to finally put to rest the spirits of The Flying Fish Lodge.

Ah, but memory is a tricky thing and reasoning with the memory is sometimes impossible.

Lisa Casey Perry is a writer, political junkie, and contributing editor of *Southern Cooking* at Suite101.com. She is the author of numerous short stories and political essays. Born and raised in Texas, she married her childhood sweetheart in 1995, sculptor David Perry. Together they have five children and six grandchildren who make every day an unpredictable adventure.

The Thin One

Jean S. Munro

When I was a child, our family home was a flat in a Glasgow tenement. Commercial premises occupied the ground floor of the building. The three upper floors each had three residential flats, all accessed from one communal stairway. On each half landing there was a large window that flooded the stairway with natural light during daylight hours. In the evening, electricity provided illumination.

The flat immediately below ours was home to three middle-aged people, two brothers, both bachelors, and their widowed sister who kept house for them. They had come over to Scotland from Ireland many years earlier but had never lost their lovely lilting Irish accents.

The sister was a quiet, gentle woman and an excellent housekeeper who kept everything in the house that could be polished, polished. The brothers were as unalike as it is possible for brothers to be. One was a short, plump, jolly man with a hail-fellow-well-met attitude toward others. The other brother was tall, rake thin, and as quiet as his brother was talkative.

In those days in Scotland, neighbors never addressed each other by their first names; it was always Mr., Mrs., or Miss. Having two men living on the same stairway with the same surname was potentially confusing. The neighbors had solved this problem by referring, amongst themselves, to one brother as The Thin One, while the other brother was simply The Other One.

The Thin One was employed by a local engineering firm and he worked shifts. His work patterns meant that I saw more of him than I did of the other two, and I would regularly meet him on the stairs when I was returning from school in the afternoon and he was on his way to begin the back shift. When he was on night shift, we met going in the opposite direction, he coming in and I setting out for school. We always exchanged a few words in these encounters, usually about the weather, school, my dog, or my cat. In the world of my childhood, he was in the category of nice, friendly grown-up.

One day I came home from school and Mother told me, "The Thin One is ill. His sister called the doctor."

"What's wrong with him?" I wanted to know.

"The doctor is not sure. He is having tests done."

In the days that followed, Mother began spending more and more time in the flat downstairs.

"I was sitting with him to give his sister a chance to rest," she would say, or "I was doing the ironing," or "I was cooking a meal for them." I was happy to agree when Mother volunteered me to do some of their shopping, collect prescriptions from the chemist, and so on. I added the Thin One's name to my nightly prayers, asking God to make him better soon.

One afternoon when I returned from school, Mother was at the door, having been watching for me from the window. She grasped my school satchel from me.

"Quick," she said, "run to the chapel. The Thin One wants a priest. Hurry!"

We were Protestants but I knew that the priests lived in a house next to the chapel and I set off as fast as I could. As I ran, I began to wonder what I would do if all the priests were already out visiting other people.

The priests' housekeeper rushed to the door in answer to my frantic ringing of the doorbell. I had barely enough breath left to gasp out the message. She disappeared inside and reappeared immediately with one of the priests. He asked no questions, just grabbed his hat and jacket from the hallstand and we were off, the priest struggling into his jacket as we went.

I was too young to realize the significance of this sudden call for the priest.

A couple of days later I was going upstairs on my way home from school when I heard footsteps and looked up. It was the Thin One!

"You're better!" I exclaimed, both astonished and delighted to see him.

We met in front of the big window and I noticed how pale he was. He had no color at all. He was wearing his working clothes. Surely he wasn't going back to work already? I wondered if the priest had prayed over him and made him better, like Jesus did when he was on Earth. Perhaps my prayers had been answered!

The Thin One stood there smiling.

"Will you be all right going back to work?" I asked. He nodded, but didn't say anything. "I'm so glad you're better," I said. He nodded again, still smiling, then turned and as he always did, raised his left hand in a farewell gesture as he made his way down the remaining stairs. I watched until he was out of sight, then went on upstairs.

Mother was out but like most Glasgow children in those days I had a Yale key on a cord round my neck and I let myself into the flat. I had scarcely time to hug my dog, put away my satchel, and hang up my coat when Mother came in.

"I was downstairs," she said. "I heard our door close and I knew you were home from school."

"It's great the Thin One's better," I said.

"Better!" exclaimed my Mother.

I explained that I had just met him on the stairs and that I was surprised he was in his working clothes and going back to work so soon. As I spoke I noticed that Mother was gripping the kitchen table so hard her knuckles were white. So was her face. She sat down suddenly.

"What's wrong?" I asked.

"Sit down," said Mother, very gently. "Tell me exactly what happened on the stairs."

I told her.

She sat silent for some time, then said, "I don't understand this. The Thin One is dead."

"Dead! He can't be! I saw him! I talked to him!"

"Yes," she agreed, "and from what you say you must have seen him seconds after he died."

"So that was his ghost leaving the building?"

"I don't know."

Mother and I talked for a long time. She ordered me not to tell anyone I had seen the Thin One. She was sure people would not believe me. Some would think I was mad, others that I was making it up, but her main concern was for his sister and brother, knowing how upset they would be should they find out.

I obeyed Mother and told no one about that encounter on the stairs, but I thought about it a lot. Until that day I had thought of ghosts as indistinct figures shrouded in mist and confined to ruined castles and graveyards. It came as a shock to realize that ghosts could appear in broad daylight and look perfectly normal!

Jean S. Munro was born and brought up in Glasgow. She worked in the Democratic Republic of Congo in Central Africa where she ran the laboratory services in a mission hospital way out in the Bush. It was while Jean was in Africa that she started writing. After twelve years in Africa she returned to the United Kingdom and specialized in electron microscopy in Glasgow Royal, continuing to write in her spare time. Eventually she had to choose between writing and electron microscopy. Much as she loved her work, she loved writing more and resigned her post. She left city life for the majestic grandeur of Argyllshire scenery. Shortly afterward, Glasgow University asked her to design courses in creative writing and offered her the post of part-time lecturer in creative writing in Argyllshire. Jean has many short stories and articles published in the U.S., Canada, the U.K., Spain, and Australia. She also has fourteen short books published in Zambia, Africa, by Copperbelt Christian Publications, three devotional books published in the U.K., and an African adventure book for nine- to eleven-year-olds published by Internet publisher www.e-booksonline.net.

The Water Ghost of #35

Michelle Porter

Growing up in New England, I am familiar with ghostly tales of haunted houses, those old family homes still visited by their former occupants, many of whom did not leave this world in a manner entirely of their choosing.

Life in old New England was very harsh to those who settled here, and perhaps it was hardest on those who built their homes on the coast and made their living by the sea.

In the early 1990s, I chose to rent a home in the seafaring port of Gloucester, Massachusetts. I lived on a street that used to be termed "Captain's Row," a short street lined with three-story structures all similar in style. These were built at the turn of the century to house the families of the Gloucester fishermen, who mainly rented the dwellings within walking distance of the town's port. Many of those men of the sea never came back, leaving their families to wonder and grieve.

As with all the houses there, they had been converted to units of two or three apartments by the time I moved in. I was on the middle, second floor of #35.

I loved that place! Bright and sunny, it had lots of charm. From the carefully chosen wallpaper and original wainscoting in the kitchen to the authentic nautical touches placed here and there: A ship's wheel framed the overhead light. An electrified starboard lamp guided my outside steps. A board washed from the sea indicated the house number.

About three months after moving in, I was in the shower early one evening, rinsing the shampoo from my hair, when the bathroom light went out.

"Darn," I fussed aloud, "I've blown a fuse." There was enough light coming through the window so I could see to finish up and get out of the water. Then I noticed that the kitchen light still shone underneath the bathroom door. Strange, I thought. A fuse would have darkened the entire side of the apartment. Suspecting a friend might have come over and was playing a joke on me, I threw on my robe and opened the bathroom door with a hearty "Ha ha, very funny." But no one answered me except my cat, who prowled her empty food dish, reminding me it was time for dinner.

The light switch to the bath was located outside the bathroom door about 5 feet up from the floor, in the kitchen. The light switch was in the off position. I flicked it up and, voilà, on went the bathroom light once again. Then I looked down. There was a puddle of water on the kitchen floor about 2 feet in diameter. Nearly perfectly round and not trickling off as it might have given that the kitchen floor had a gentle slope to it. I wondered and mopped up the puddle.

Over the course of the next few months, this happened time and again. Same puddle on the floor in the same location as before. One evening, in early June, this strange phenomenon occurred while a friend was in the living room watching TV. I'd told him about my encounters and I think he thought I was just "spinning a yarn." But now he was about to be faced with the indisputable facts.

Reeling from the kitchen, I asked him if he'd seen or heard anything that could account for the water on the floor. He replied that he had heard nothing unusual. "You must have heard something," I almost demanded, slightly annoyed that he'd just sat there while someone was dumping water on my kitchen floor. I looked around, bewildered. Alex Trebek continued reading the answers on *Jeopardy*. The cat was curled up on the sofa. Everything was "normal." Except for the fact that I'd experienced another bathroom blackout and the unexplained appearance of water that followed.

My friend was as baffled as I was as we stared down at the puddle of water on the floor. "Smell it," he suggested. I kneeled down and put my face close to the puddle. "Smells kinda salty," I said. He reached down, stuck his finger in the water, and put it to his mouth. "This is seawater!" he exclaimed, jumping back a bit, perhaps getting a little spooked. I did the same, and it was, indeed, salt water.

My "saltwater ghost" paid me a visit on two occasions after that and then abruptly stopped. I remained at #35 for four more years before moving again. I must say though, that despite the inconvenience of a wet floor, I missed the presence and often wonder what was meant by it. Was it the spirit of some young man lost at sea? Did he come back to his home on "Captain's Row" disturbed to find that it was now hacked into apartments and had indoor plumbing? Had his hands once gripped the wheel that now adorned my living room in an effort to navigate his vessel through rough New England seas? I would never have my answer.

I said goodbye to my water spirit when I realized it was gone, wishing it a bon voyage and clear sail through the realm of the other world.

Michelle Porter was born and raised in Newton, Massachusetts. After many years as a professional cook, she pursued a degree in Food Science and Nutrition from the Essex Agricultural & Technical Institute in Danvers. She now works in customer service and also offers personal nutritional counseling while pursuing her lifelong love of writing. Michelle is an avid reader and has been writing for pleasure and personal exploration ever since she could first hold a pencil. She believes in storytelling — stories that are passed on by people in families, neighborhoods, and towns that are recounted until they become sort of legends. That's the magic of a story. The story she has presented here is true. Though she searched for related stories regarding her home, she found nothing to authenticate this one. However, Michelle keeps an open mind, and there's a first time for everything. That's how a story starts.

Protective Spirits

Mitchel Whitington

We knew that our house, The Grove, was haunted when we bought it. The previous owner told us, just like the owner before had told him. Odd things started happening around the place almost immediately. We heard footsteps across empty rooms, the sound of rustling skirts filled the side gallery when no one was there, and my wife and I have both seen a man in a black suit who seems to linger in the garden before fading away.

People who come to visit when we've been gone have told us some of the most interesting stories. A friend enjoying a walk through the garden while waiting for us to get home reported seeing the face of a woman peeking out of one of the windows at him. Another friend waited on the front porch, certain we were inside because she heard furniture being moved around in the parlor; we weren't there, of course. A family member passed by, saw that our front gate was unlatched, and walked across the footbridge to latch it. The closer he got to the house, the dizzier he became. A ringing in his ears got louder and louder, to the point where he couldn't stand it. When he reached the gate and latched it, everything instantly cleared up.

There are literally dozens of stories like these. The spirits at The Grove are very protective.

One of the most interesting things that we've experienced happened in October of 2002. We'd been invited to a surprise birthday party one evening, and I planned to take a few plates of my special chicken wings. The night before, I prepared batches of three favorite kinds: bourbon wings, lemon wings, and chipotle pepper wings. The best thing about these recipes is that you mix the sauce ingredients together the night before, and simply let the wings marinate overnight in the refrigerator. An hour before it's time to serve them, all you have to do is pop them in the oven and let them cook! It couldn't be easier — or so I thought.

The hour of the party was approaching, so I turned the oven dial to 375 degrees, and began laying the wings out on baking pans. I'd given the oven about fifteen minutes to warm up, which I assumed to be plenty of time. The gas oven/stove looked almost as old as the house did, but we'd found it to be functional and assumed that it would work well enough until we started remodeling the kitchen. That day, however, when I opened the oven door to put the wings in, it was as cold as a fall morning.

I remembered that we'd had gas heaters installed in the house the week before, and one was in the kitchen. The serviceman who did the work had shut the gas off for safety. I realized the oven pilot light must not have been relit, something that would certainly be easy for me to fix. I found a flashlight and opened the lower front panel of the oven where the pilot was, and caught the unmistakable odor of natural gas.

We didn't have any matches in the house, only one long lighter wand that we used for candles occasionally. I grabbed it out of the basket on the island in the center of the kitchen and kneeled back down in front of the oven. I was more than a little bothered by the gas odor, and I hesitated before pulling the trigger to light the wand. In fact, I finally turned around and laid it on one of the lower shelves of the kitchen island while I inspected the pilot chamber again with the flashlight.

Time ticked away, and the possibility of taking half-cooked chicken wings and being late to the party loomed on the horizon. I distinctly remember thinking to myself, "I hope I don't blow this place sky-high!" Still, the pilot light had to be lit, so I turned around to pick up the lighter wand. It was gone.

Even though I knew exactly where I'd laid it down, I started searching the entire island, then the kitchen, and finally the rest of the house itself. My wife started to worry about the time as well, and when I told her what had happened she joined me in the search. For the next thirty minutes, we turned the place upside down. The lighter wand had apparently vanished.

Now, I'm as bad as anyone about putting something down and not remembering where I put it, but in this particular case everything was very cut and dried. I was on my hands and knees in front of the stove, and reached around to put the wand on a shelf of the island. I wasn't walking around, I wasn't moving through the house. I knew exactly where I'd put the lighter. We were baffled.

Finally, my wife suggested we light a taper candle on the flames from the stove, then use the candle to light the oven's pilot light. That's exactly what I did — since the panel door had been open for the half-hour while we'd been searching the house, the pilot chamber no longer smelled like gas. The oven came on, the wings baked, and we made it to the party just in time. And the chicken wings were a huge hit!

I wrote the missing lighter wand off as just one of the many unusual experiences associated with the house, and the next week I picked up a new one at the grocery store. We didn't think anything else about it until the next Wednesday evening. I was in the kitchen again, and my wife was in the front East Parlor that we use as a dining room. There is a large, 1920s buffet cabinet there that we'd had for a couple of months. She opened it to get some dishes out because we were having friends over for dinner.

She called me, and I could tell by the tone of her voice that something was wrong. I dashed to the East Parlor, and she stood there with one of the buffet doors open. Inside, lying on a stack of dishes, was the missing lighter wand.

I always try to be skeptical when analyzing something that seems supernatural, but in this case, I was out of answers. Neither one of us had looked inside the buffet since we first stacked the dishes there a few months before. But even if we went through it on a daily basis, it was on the opposite end of the house from the kitchen where the lighter wand disappeared.

The only explanation that I have is that the protective spirits of The Grove who are so adept at watching out for strangers got a little nervous when I was about to light an oven when I smelled gas, and moved the lighter wand to give the gas time to dissipate. In any case, I'm grateful to them — and I'll sleep a little better knowing that they're so vigilant.

Mitchel Whitington is a writer with comedic-fiction credits such as *Uncle Bubba's Chicken Wing Fling*, and non-fiction haunted travel guides, the latest of which is *Ghosts of North Texas*. *Spirits of East Texas* and *Untold Tales of Texas Ghosts* will be released in 2003 and 2004 respectively. Mitchel and his wife Tami are the owners of The Grove, a 150-year-old house in Jefferson, Texas, that has been called the "most haunted house in the most haunted city in Texas."

Enlightening Visit

Bobbie Christmas

My sister Sandi and I had a close relationship. Although two years apart in age, we acted more like friends. We played together all day, cuddled in bed at night, and woke up to start all over again. When I reached first grade, she, the expert third-grader, walked me to and from school, from the first day on.

One of our favorite games involved dress up, with a twist. We did not dress ourselves. Ever the fashion designer, she dressed me up like a model. Afterwards, she faced me toward a mirror and whispered over my shoulder, "Bobbie, look at you! You're so pretty. You're so smart. I love you."

She was tall, slender, outgoing, and naturally beautiful. I was short, plump, shy, and plain. Her words sounded good to me, even though I had difficulty internalizing them. Through sheer repetition, she slowly got through to me.

We didn't know the term "self-esteem" in those days, but my confidence developed through her loving support and encouragement. She never failed to find an opportunity to tell me of my greatness. When she reached high school and aspired to be a cheerleader, she practiced by performing cheers to me: "Two, four, six, eight, who do we appreciate? Bobbie, Bobbie, Bobbie!"

With six children, my parents stayed busy, but I did not notice the lack of individual attention from them, because I received so much unconditional love and undivided attention from my sister Sandi.

In our teen years, she introduced me to boys her age, and we often double-dated. At a time when I needed a confidante, she was a pillar. I could tell her anything, and it went no further. She confided in me as well, and I felt honored to be the keeper of her secrets. I was the only person she told about her first crush. She was the only person I told about my first kiss.

At age twenty in 1962, Sandi moved to New York. In one of her visits back to our hometown of Columbia, South Carolina, she disclosed to me that she had taken up skydiving. She warned me not to tell anyone, lest our parents forbid her to pursue the sport she loved. A phone call in late October two years later revealed all and jolted the family into reality. Sandi had fallen to her death in a skydiving accident. She was one of the first women in America to die in such an accident, and the news spread worldwide. An uncle overseas saw it in an Italian newspaper. Sandi had become a statistic, a news story.

Devastated, I had lost not only my sister but also my best friend.

My younger sister, at age fourteen, still needed guidance. I could not reach out to her for friendship.

My oldest sister lived 500 miles away with a husband and three daughters. We seemed worlds apart, physically and emotionally.

My cousin, a few months older than me, had moved to Florida.

My parents, tied up in their own grief, could not console me.

At twenty, I had no one to turn to.

Feeling mortal for the first time, I took inventory of my life, fearing I might also die at age twenty-two. If I had only two years to live, how did I want to live it? What did I want to accomplish? Sad that Sandi had not married or had children, I set out on a mission to get married and have a child before I turned twenty-two. Following our cultural tradition, I would honor the dead by naming my child after her.

As if scripted, my days played out as planned. I moved to a larger city to start a new life, with the hidden agenda of shopping for a husband. In less than a year, I met a suitable guy who asked me to marry him. I rushed him to the altar, knowing I had to get pregnant and have a child as soon as possible.

Everything happened on schedule. Before I turned twenty-two, I gave birth to a healthy son I named Sandy. My only problem: I did not have a healthy marriage. The person I thought had been suitable turned out to be a tyrant, a philanderer, dangerously controlling, involved in illegal activities, and to make matters worse, he had no feelings whatsoever for our son. I wanted to leave my husband, but I had no car, no job, and no money, and I had an infant. What could I do? I did not think I had any options other than to stay in a bad marriage.

One day, my older brother came to town on business. I had never confided in him before, but when he arrived, I told him of my situation. He, in turn, told my parents.

Mother called to ask if I wanted to leave. I said, "Yes, but I don't know how. I can't afford —"

She interrupted, "Come back home. You can stay with us until you get on your feet."

Those words might have been consoling to most women in my circumstances, but I could not admit defeat. I would have to divulge my gross error in judgment. Everyone would know I was not the adult I had tried to be.

Most of my acquaintances looked down on divorced women, as if they had broken an unwritten code of conduct. I did not want to stay married to an ogre, but I also did not want to incur scorn from my elders and peers. I could not find the nerve to go back to my parents' house with a baby. Adding to my quandary, in the 1960s, no one in my family had ever gotten a divorce.

I mulled over my choices, none of them clear-cut. I wanted to maintain my dignity, yet I could not, no matter whether I stayed or got a divorce. I wanted my freedom, but at what price? How could I support an infant when I had no marketable skills? In my last job, I had earned only forty dollars a week. Day care cost about thirty-five dollars a week.

That night, instead of packing to leave, I lay in bed alone, my husband gone, as usual. I mulled over my life and tried to find the strength to do the right thing. I needed to save my son and myself from a fiend who became worse with each passing week, but how would I face the ridicule, disapproval, and disdain sure to come my way in my hometown? I could not do it by myself.

Ping! As if someone had flipped a light switch, a ball of light appeared at the far right end of my bed, below where my husband's feet should have been. I thought at first that a car had pulled up outside with the headlights on, but the bright glow floated and bounced a little in the air, slightly above the level of the mattress. The illumination moved, almost flowed, around the bottom of the footboard. I watched in awe as it turned the corner at my feet and came up to my side. At the moment my curiosity almost gave way to panic, I heard my dead sister's voice, spoken directly into my ear. It was not a whisper, and it wasn't a shout. In a normal tone, she said my first name. She spoke it as a question: "Bobbie?"

I sat up, and the shine disappeared.

"Bobbie?" She spoke in a voice I had not heard in two years but had no trouble recognizing.

"Bobbie?" I thought about her inflection. I knew it meant something. I took a deep breath. I realized she meant, "Bobbie, can't you see you're strong enough to handle anything?" My sister always made me believe in myself, and once again, in her own way, she relayed what I most needed to hear.

I stayed awake all night, finally knowing what I had to do. When my husband slipped into the bed in the wee hours of the morning, I acted asleep. I did not want to break the warm spell created from the love of my sister, the confidence she gave me to make a difficult decision.

The next day I left town with the dress on my back and a suitcase full of diapers. Once home, I found my family welcoming, warm, and without judgment. My life took off in a rewarding direction, as my younger brother and sister fell in love with my son and helped take care of him. We all grew closer than ever. I joined my father in his new business, and we benefited from working together. Our relationship deepened.

Eventually I remarried, when I found a man I loved and who adored my son. My new husband adopted Sandy and helped rear him to have ethics and complete confidence in himself. At thirty-six, Sandy is married to his best friend and is a successful doctor of veterinary medicine.

From another realm, my sister had told me in my worst hour that I had the strength I needed and all would be well.

Sandi never again appeared to me as a ball of light or an audible voice. Perhaps she never deemed it necessary, because I've never again lacked the confidence that I could make difficult decisions. If my courage should ever fail me, though, she's out there, and she'll remind me of what I already know.

Bobbie Christmas is the owner of Zebra Communications, a literary services firm in metro Atlanta that offers editing, ghostwriting, and submissions services. She drives a zebra-striped car, a terrible getaway car for bank heists, so she must by necessity write and edit for a living. Her story recounts her first supernatural encounter. Bobbie has spent more than 30 years as a professional writer and editor. She is the author of an upcoming book, *Rev Up Your Writing!* She is a past president of the Georgia Writers Association and is on its Board of Advisors and is a past vice president of the South Carolina Writers Workshop. Bobbie is the leader of The Writers Network and director of the *Lessons Learned* anthology competition for The Knowledge Shop, Chapter 11 Discount Book Stores, and the Georgia Writers Association. She welcomes questions and comments at www.zebraeditor.com.

The Brown Lady of Raynham Hall

Docia Williams

D o I believe in ghosts? You bet I do! I never actually went out hunting for one, but purely by accident, or perhaps, on her part, by design, I did meet up with a very famous ghost back when I was a young woman living in England. It all began when my first husband, Stanley Southworth, then an Air Force lieutenant, was transferred from Nashville, Tennessee, to England. It was May of 1955. The rural area where we were stationed was in Norfolk County, and there was base housing for only senior officers and their families. We were forced to live on the local economy. We found a beautiful flat in a huge four-story manor house situated on a large estate overlooking a small lake. It was an idyllic setting for a young couple like us to call "home."

Raynham Hall was the ancestral seat of the Townshend family. The Marquis and Marchioness Townshend rented out a few apartments in their large house and adjoining converted carriage house to American families. I was told the British were having a difficult time paying estate taxes in postwar England and this was an added source of income.

Our flat was on the top floor of the manor, which was a red brick building designed by the architect Inigo Jones in 1620. It was a sturdy building, with high ceilings, curving marble stairways, and echoing hallways. We entered the building from the rear, through a courtyard where we parked our little English Triumph TR2 sports car. The entry hall was centered with a large table. Off to one side was a dark hallway leading to a chamber where the coal was kept. On the other side were the back stairs, which we used to reach our quarters. Our corner apartment consisted of four large rooms: a living room, a dining room, a bedroom with a commodious bathroom, which quite obviously had been carved out of a portion of the bedroom, and a sizeable kitchen overlooking the front of the estate. It was sparsely but adequately furnished. There was a large fireplace in three of the rooms, and a small electric heater took the chill off of the bathroom. All in all, it was a beautiful place to live and, fortunately, was affordable for us on a lieutenant's pay.

The place was chilly, even though it was May when we moved there. I presumed this was because it was an old building, and the ceilings were fourteen feet high. Now, looking back, I believe it was cold for other reasons. The first inkling I had that anything "different" might be going on occurred one night soon after we moved in. My pilot husband was away on an overnight mission. I'd just received a large envelope of news clippings from my mother, back home in Texas. She clipped articles from the hometown paper she thought would interest me, and stuffed them in big manila envelopes that she sent to me once or twice a month. They were a wonderful link to home. This particular night I was sitting up in bed, reading the clippings, with a blanket over my legs. There was no fire laid in the fireplace, but the nights were always a bit nippy there in Norfolk. Suddenly, the door to our bedroom opened, all of its own accord, and then a draft passed right by my bed, with a definite drop in temperature. And there was a strange odor. It was like a root cellar or newly turned earth. It reminded me of the smell of the old storm cellar at my grandmother's house in north Texas. It literally permeated the room.

Then whatever "it" was that had entered the room pulled open the drapes that were drawn over a quartet of large windows. These drapes were of burgundy velvet, lined, and were extremely heavy. I had to yank the curtain-pull hard to open and close them. Centered between the four floor-to-ceiling windows was a French door that opened onto a little mock balcony. These doors flew open (and I knew they had been locked), and "it" apparently went out onto the balcony! I just sat, immobile, in the bed, while all this took place. It couldn't have taken more than a minute or two, but it was a very unnerving experience. Finally, I got out of bed, and hesitantly walked over to the French doors. I peeked out on the little balcony, knowing full well I wouldn't see anything, then closed and locked the doors and closed the heavy drapes. I went all over the flat and turned on every light. I sat up most of the night, too frightened and puzzled to fall asleep.

When my husband returned the next night I told him what had occurred. He didn't believe me. He asked if I had been nipping at the cooking sherry!

A couple of weeks later, when I was again alone at night, a wispy, vaporous shape of "something" came drifting out of the fireplace, floated across the room, and disappeared when it reached the draperies over the bank of windows. There was no fire lit in the grate, so I knew it couldn't be smoke. Again, I was "spooked," but still didn't know what it was, and didn't really think of ghosts, per se, since I had never experienced a supernatural happening in my life.

A short time later, we had callers one Sunday afternoon. My husband's former commander at Donaldson Air Force Base, Col. Tom Schofield, had arrived at Sculthorpe, and he and his lovely wife, Beulah, called on us. They had scarcely taken a seat in our living room when Colonel Tom, as I called him, said, "When are you kids getting out of this place?" I can vividly recall him saying this. We said, "Why, we've just settled in here." He said he didn't like the place, that there was something just not quite right about it, and he would feel much better if we moved elsewhere as soon as possible. He said he was extremely uncomfortable there. This was a senior officer, much older than we were, and a decorated combat veteran. Even though I had not been able to, I think the colonel got my husband's attention!

There were several young American couples who lived in the converted carriage house adjacent to the manor house with whom we had become acquainted. We would often get together and play bridge in the evenings. None of us had much money, and this was our chief source of socializing. But after one visit to our flat, they all said, "You can come to our place. We really don't like going up there to your flat."

One night while I was taking a bath in the big, roomy bathroom off of our bedroom, I suddenly heard a babble of voices in the wall. I judged they were coming from the corridor outside of our flat. The place was always very quiet, as Lord and Lady Townshend and their family were in Switzerland that summer, and the servants lived in small cottages down the lane from the main house. Most nights we were there alone, in that huge, forty-four room mansion. Sometimes the estate agent, Mrs. Severn, spent the night there in a flat on the same floor as ours, but she was the only person I ever saw. Now, I thought, there must be a party going on. I hastily dried off, got dressed, and stuck my head outside our doorway. The hallway was dark and deserted. It was not until later, much later, that I learned that spirits often manifest themselves by having unintelligible conversations in the walls.

Finally, very late one moonlit night, my "flying warrior" arrived home around midnight. He was visibly shaken! The hair was standing up on his arms and the back of his neck. He said "something" had passed him on the stairs, although he had seen nothing, and the stairs, illuminated by a skylight at the top, were clearly visible. He said, "We are going to look for whatever it was." I said "We?" He said that was right, he and I together were going to look for what passed him on the stairs. He took a flashlight and his service revolver with him and insisted I go with him. I realized, after several months of his ignoring my reports of all sorts of eerie things going on, that he had finally, like Napoleon, met his Waterloo. We looked all over the old house, even going into the dark coal cellar, and found nothing. But he was becoming convinced there really was something there. After a few other unnerving events took place, he finally said, "It's going to be very cold this winter, and I think we ought to look for a cozy little cottage somewhere that won't be so hard to heat."

We did find a cottage in a small village some miles from Raynham Hall, and never went back there. I had learned just prior to our leaving, from the old butler, that the place was haunted, big time. In fact, the Brown Lady of Raynham Hall is one of England's most famous ghosts and has been haunting her bedchamber of the old hall for many years, since her death in 1726. I believe our bedroom was where she died. She was Dorothy Walpole Townshend. Her portrait, which was sold at Christie's back in 1904, pictured a lovely young woman with beautiful shining eyes, dressed in brown with yellow trimmings and a large ruff around her neck, in the style of the day. The portrait looked lovely in ordinary light, but when seen by candlelight it took on a sinister appearance. The flesh seemed to recede from her eyes and they became big hollows, and the face resembled a skull. It is said that when King George (the father of England's Queen Elizabeth) was a young prince, he visited the Townshends for a weekend hunting party. He was given the most elegant of the guest chambers, called the "royal chamber." There, he was awakened from a sound sleep by the appearance of the Brown Lady standing at the foot of his bed. There are still bullet holes in the room where the prince riddled the wall with his pistol to frighten the apparition away. He didn't stay for the hunt. The next morning he told his valet it was time to pack up and be out of there!

Now, some forty-eight years later, looking back on those days at Raynham, I think I would be more fascinated than frightened. Why, the Brown Lady has actually been featured in a History Channel documentary about England's haunted houses. It's really rather special to think my first indoctrination into the spirit world was in the company of a really famous ghost. I believe she is a lonely, sad little soul who has never found eternal rest. However, at that time in my life I was scared out of my wits! Even now, when I think of Raynham Hall, I get little shivers up and down my spine.

Docia Schultz Williams is a professional writer, lecturer, and certified professional tour guide. She makes her home in San Antonio, Texas.

She has conducted tours all over the United States and to many foreign destinations, including Europe, China, Africa, Canada, and South America. She resided for a number of years in both England and Spain where she pursued her interest in the arts, history, and antiques. She is a member of the Professional Tour Guides Association of San Antonio.

Co-author of the book, *Spirits of San Antonio and South Texas*, she is also the author of *Ghosts Along the Texas Coast*, *Phantoms of the Plains*, *When Darkness Falls*, *Best Tales of Texas Ghosts*, *The History and Mystery of the Menger Hotel*, and *Exploring San Antonio with Children, A Guide for Family Activities*. She originated a nighttime tour, "The Spirits of San Antonio Tour," featuring the most haunted spots in town, which received the prestigious "Gemmy" award from the Midwest Travel Writers' Association for being one of the country's truly unique travel experiences. A frequent club and convention speaker, she has appeared in many Texas cities. She is also a featured cruise lecturer with the Norwegian and Commodore cruise lines. She will soon have another book ready for press, much to the delight of her readers and her publishing house.

The Mischievous Little Girl

George E. Banks, Jr.

I t was an early summer evening and my wife and daughter and I were pulling weeds around our mobile home. Our small dog, Shadow, was "helping" us by nosing around and pestering us for attention.

Suddenly Shadow bolted for the other side of our home and we soon heard him growling and barking furiously. Cassie, our eight-year-old daughter, took off after the dog.

"I wonder if Shadow is barking at the little girl again," my wife, Sandra, mused to herself.

"Who knows? Does sound like the bark he gets when she shows up," I said. We got up and went to investigate.

When we got around the house, there was Shadow, jumping up, circling, and barking at something only he could see. To us it looked as if he were attacking nothing more than air. This was something that we had seen the dog do many times and were not surprised at his antics.

"It's her again, isn't it daddy?" Cassie asked me.

"Don't know, kiddo. Maybe."

For almost six years, since the day our mobile home was delivered to our rural property, we had been plagued by many mysterious occurrences. Common household items, books — almost anything — on occasion would be moved around or thrown to the floor. Sometimes something would just disappear and be gone for weeks, only to show up again just where it had been left at the time of its disappearance.

Moved or missing things weren't the only strange and unexplainable things happening. All three of us had often heard the voice of a little girl in different places in our home. Sometimes she would laugh or cry, but mostly she would sing or we would hear simple words or snatches of what seemed to be her side of a conversation with someone else. We had come to learn that whenever we heard the little girl's voice there was sure to be a few days of irritating pranks to follow.

We never saw the little girl but apparently our dog could, or could sense her in some way, because many times he would circle and snap and bark at some unseen (to us) presence. Eventually this unseen presence would move off, sometimes up a wall with Shadow vainly trying to follow it.

When we first began experiencing these strange events, we were afraid of what was happening, as anyone would be, but over time we lost our fear. This "spirit" had never actually harmed us. She just seemed content to keep playing her annoying tricks on us. We soon got used to things being tossed about or hidden. It was a bit frightening, however, when she would begin singing or laughing in the middle of the night or start talking during our quiet reading time.

About a year ago I decided to find out something about our mysterious houseguest if I could. I thought a good place to start would be at the dealership where we had bought the mobile home. The home had been two years old when we bought it and we had lived in it almost six years. I wasn't sure if the dealer would keep records that long but I thought it was worth a try.

The older man who owned the dealership was pleasant and friendly, and I told him the story of the little girl who was an unseen but apparently constant tenant of our home whether we liked it or not. He laughed at my tale but was more than eager to see if he could find the records of our mobile home. Thankfully, he was thorough and meticulous in his recordkeeping and though it took a while he eventually found the file on our mobile home purchase and sat down at his desk to read it.

As he perused the file, his perpetual smile began to fade. After he had read the last page, he closed the file and looked at me with nervous uncertainty.

"Mr. Banks, I remember your home now. We had a rough time trying to get it cleaned up. I laughed a few minutes ago at what you told me but I'm not laughing now because there just might be something to your story after all."

Although reluctant to do so, after I pressed him for details he finally told me the story of our mobile home.

The original family who had purchased the home had it set up outside of Fort Worth, Texas. After just eighteen months of living in the new home, a weekend of bloody horror had happened. The man of the house, for some inexplicable reason, had erupted into a screaming frenzy and brutally murdered his wife and little girl. After the heinous carnage was finished, he then took his own life. A few months after the killing the mobile home dealer had bought the home at auction and had it moved to his lot for sale.

When I got home I told Sandra and Cassie the story and they were as stunned as I was when I first heard it. Was the voice we kept hearing that of the little girl who had been murdered by her daddy? If so, would she forever stay in the home instead of moving on to another spiritual plane? Was there anything that we could do to help her?

These were questions that we just could not answer no matter how much we thought about the situation or however much research we devoted to finding the answers.

We are still awakened at night by her voice and things still get moved around or hidden on us. Shadow still chases and barks at a presence that only he can sense. Perhaps it actually is the spirit of the murdered little girl who still plays the mischievous tricks on us and sings to us or laughs in such a soft pretty voice. We do not know for certain who or what it really is and probably never will. We have no fear of this young spirit, if that is what it is, only sorrow and pity. We have come to love this constant presence. Whenever something is missing or a few things are tossed around or moved out of place, we no longer get angry or irritated. When we are startled by her small voice in the night, we simply wish her young spirit well and answer her, calling out with a prayer for her peaceful rest and a final release from her horrible nightmare.

George E. Banks, Jr., lives with his wife and daughter in southeast rural Oklahoma where he writes short stories and novels about ghosts, supernatural encounters, horror, and science fiction. He also writes e-books on the same subjects as well as natural living topics and science. His novels include *False Dawn*, a story of supernatural horror on post-apocalyptic Earth, *The Empty Garden*, a

George E. Banks, Jr.

science fiction story about an alien ghost ship found by a crew
of space scavengers, and a nonfiction book titled *Road Map for
the Astral Traveler.*

A Mother's Day Gift For My Sister

Laurie Moore

"This is the operator. Would you release the line for —"

My heart went dead. Having a telephone operator cut into the line ranks right up there with a grim-faced state trooper walking up your sidewalk. The day after Mother's Day in 1994, another law student and I were comparing answers from our family law exam earlier that afternoon; instinctively, we knew the interruption meant trouble, and neither of us wanted to be the recipient of bad news.

Things worked out in her favor.

Even before I heard the quiver in my stepdad's voice at the other end of the line, I knew my life would change forever.

"Come to the house. Something bad has happened."

I listened in stunned silence. My mind went through a series of mental gymnastics. Instinctively, my eyes cut to the living room, where my child watched TV, and I felt a profound sense of relief. I thought of my mother, still teaching despite her age. Almost as if he read my thoughts, I heard, "It's not your mother —"

That left my sister.

A frantic pulse throbbed in my throat.

"— it's Grant."

* * * * *

Ten pounds, ten ounces. Plump skin, no wrinkles.

It is often said that the biggest babies in the hospital are the prettiest. The first time I saw my nephew, I marveled at the sheer size of him. As a day-old baby he had already outgrown the zero-to-six-month clothes my sister's friends brought to the baby shower. It pleased me that twenty years up the road, I could have season tickets on the fifty-yard line for all the Dallas Cowboy games, compliments of our little linebacker.

But nineteen Mother's Days had come and gone. Along the way, I reconciled myself to the fact that if I wanted football tickets, I'd have to buy them. With his twentieth birthday only days away, Grant, an honor student at Southwestern University, already had his sights set on the law.

I wondered on the short drive over to my parents' house if he'd been involved in a car wreck. But my stepfather hadn't said anyone died; he'd only prepared me for something so bad that we needed to come together as a family.

Halfway there, I bartered with God. The thing about God is that He already knows whether you'll keep your promises; I had an idea He saw through the flimsy ones I made, especially when I swore I'd get involved with the church I'd been absent from most of my adult life, if only He'd make things okay. Not perfect. Not great. Merely okay. I knew He knew these unrealistic vows would be broken, as certain as an unenforceable contract, but I exhausted a long list of things I would give up if only He'd keep my nephew alive.

Maybe it wasn't a car wreck.

Maybe gang members killed him.

The perfect child had no connection to that ilk, but with carjackings splashed across the front page with alarming regularity, I considered the possibility he had become a victim. I couldn't bear it if he suffered. "Please, please, please —" I caught myself wailing. The sight of my young daughter, wide-eyed and shaking, made me stop. Convinced the situation called for revenge, I pledged to turn vigilante.

Wheeling the car around the last curve, I saw my white-haired stepdad, a tall man of imposing stature, pacing the brick walk in front of their house, with his head ducked low. As I zipped into the drive and yanked up the emergency brake, he appeared, slump-shouldered, at my car door. I still had not seen my mother, and momentarily thought he had lied.

"Grant's dead."

Never in my life, had I seen my stepdad — a World War II recipient of the Distinguished Flying Cross — cry.

My dad described it as a seizure; the autopsy read cardiac arrhythmia. There was no one to blame. No one to exact revenge on. Nothing to do but sit back and watch my family fall apart. Grant had a congenital heart defect.

* * * * *

This past year, a few weeks before Christmas, I slept in Grant's bedroom. My sister, a tall, honey-blonde with large hazel eyes and olive skin that gives her an exotic appearance, poked her head inside the door to see if I needed anything.

"I do." I wondered how to begin. "I need to ask you about Grant. I need to know what he said to you on Mother's Day. If he seemed fine. If he acted sick."

I needed to know if there had been any warning.

She slipped into the room, closed the door, and delivered her response in a hushed tone.

It had surprised her to see him on Mother's Day because of his final exams. When he pulled into the drive, she offered to prepare King Ranch Casserole, a favorite of his, made with chicken, tortillas, cheese, and cream soups. Instead, Grant asked for a hot dog.

"I tried to talk him into letting me make him a real meal, but he didn't want me to go to any trouble." She fixed the hot dog and gave it to him.

He made an unexpected request. "Tell me about Griff. What was he like?"

I sat bolt upright in the bed, stunned. Grant had never met Griff. Griff was our father. He died of a heart attack when my sister and I were just little girls.

The question took my sister aback. "I told Grant to look at the picture in the hall, but he shook his head and described Daddy to a T. Grant was more interested in how Daddy acted, his mannerisms, things he would say. We talked for a long time, and I told him what I could remember. In the end, Grant said, 'That was Griff. I dreamed about him last night.'"

It seemed odd Grant should dream of our father, but my sister wrote it off as inconsequential, and reminded him of his twentieth birthday a few days away.

She said, "Come back Saturday and we'll buy you some new clothes for next semester."

He laughed. "This is the last time you're ever going to see me."

"What're you talking about?"

"I'm never going to see you again." More laughter.

"Sure you are. You're coming for your birthday."

"No, I'm not," he said through a grin. "I'm never coming back."

That was Grant's way. To joke and put people at ease. He had artfully dodged her question.

Before leaving, he picked up his little brother by the shoulders, lifted him from the floor and kissed him on the forehead. "I love you, little boy. Take care of our mother."

My sister accompanied him to the car. "About Saturday —"

"Mom, I told you, this is the last time I'll ever see you."

"Quit fooling around. I put aside some money to shop for your clothes. Are you coming or not?"

"I don't need any more clothes."

"Well, you're getting them anyway."

His mood turned serious. "Mom, you don't have to worry about money anymore." He gave her a hug and a kiss good-bye, and cut his eyes to the house and back. "I'll help you put him through college."

"What about Saturday. Will I see you?"

"No. I'm not having a birthday this year."

* * * * *

"He must have known," I said to my sister. "Why would he all of a sudden ask about Daddy?" She shook her head. Slow, deliberate shakes. "Okay, I'm not saying I believe in this, but maybe you and I should go see somebody. Ever watch those

TV shows where a psychic hosts the program?" One of her eyebrows corkscrewed. "Even if you don't believe in that kind of stuff — and I don't — the guests always seem to feel better when they leave. Maybe we should go — for the experience."

She shook her head. "I don't have to. I know he's fine."

"How do you know?"

Her voice barely rose above a whisper. "After I lost him, nothing went right. Three years after he died, I had almost completely given up. One morning, I woke up and had to drag myself out of bed to get ready for work."

To save time, she decided not to wash her hair. But once she tamed the cowlicks and brushed out the curls, it still looked unruly. Taking the brush and forcing it into her hair with bold, harsh strokes, she cursed her reflection.

"Would you look at this hair? I can't get it to do anything. I'm going to be late. Would you look at this —ing hair, Grant?"

Unexpectedly, a blast of hot air rushed past her neck like a sprite. Stunned, she held the brush aloft. Grant's laughter filled the space behind her.

"Is that you, Grant? Are you laughing at my hair? It's horrible, isn't it?"

His laughter echoed in her ears, then faded into nothing.

My sister's eyes held me transfixed. "It's enough that I know he was here. That he let me know things would turn around for me. And that he wanted me to know he's fine. That even though he's not here —" She spread her hands, palms up. "—*he's here*. Watching over me. And that's all I need to know."

* * * * *

The last time I saw my sister, I asked for permission to repeat this story. It had been told to me in confidence, and it wasn't mine to tell. I offered to change the names for confidentiality's sake, but she said no.

"Use it if you like. Maybe it'll help another mother out there. It doesn't matter what others think. Anyone who's ever lost a child will understand."

Merry Laureen Moore, "Laurie" to her friends, is a former police officer, district attorney investigator, and reserve deputy constable. She is a native Texan, currently practicing law in the Cultural District of "Cowtown." Writing is her passion. She wrote her first mystery on blue construction paper, with an orange crayon, at the age of six and gave it to her father for his birthday. Laurie's first two novels, *Constable's Run* and *The Lady Godiva Murder*, were released in 2002 by Five Star, an imprint of Gale Group. The second in each series, *Constable's Apprehension* and *The Wild Orchid Society*, have release dates of 2003 and 2004, respectively. "A Mother's Day Gift For My Sister" is her first published short story. Laurie is a member of the DFW Writer's Workshop, where she serves on the Board of Directors. She resides in Fort Worth with her daughter, two bad Siamese, and a Welsh Corgi, and is still a licensed, commissioned peace officer.

The Hills Are with Me Always

Mona D. Sizer

The mighty Arkansas River cuts a deep canyon through the state named for it. Between the Ozarks in the northwest and the Ouachitas in the south runs the small tributary Petit Jean, named for a French explorer's daughter whom legend says drowned in its rippling stream. In that secluded valley, folks don't put much stock in the legend because her little ghost has never been seen.

On either side of the narrow valley, the hills — Magazine, Poteau, and Blue Mountains — rise to three thousand feet. In the winter the clouds sit on their shoulders and the fogs rise out of the hollows. At dawn every stock pond has its own pale wraiths creeping out across the meadows clad in ghostly garments. Then the sun bursts over the ridgeline and everything returns to light and brilliant color.

A hundred years ago, it was a country of cousins where a woman was related to everyone she met either on her mother's or her father's side. Everyone knew and helped everyone else. Moreover, they all calmly accepted the spirits of their dead that walked among them, unseen perhaps but offering aid and comfort in time of need. And the old folks assured us all, "The circle will never be broken." Every time my grandmother took me back to our home place, we visited the cemetery. Even as a child I felt comfortable there, as if I were welcomed.

We'd walk up the hill to a grove of cedar trees at least a hundred years old. There my great-grandparents were buried with all the little children around them who'd died young — eight little graves and tiny tombstones, leaving only five children to grow to maturity.

They say that those little children were in Heaven, and Heaven is a beautiful place — perhaps an Arkansas cemetery with hundred-year-old cedar trees beneath which their spirits rest. I felt them as surely as my grandmother did. The spirits were part of the plan of things.

My grandmother knew they were there because she'd encountered one. In that cemetery, she told me about the night she met one. And for the first time in that cemetery, I shuddered. Cold chills ran up and down my arms and set me looking over my shoulder as the wind soughed through the branches. Thereafter she told it every time we came to the cemetery, so I would be sure to remember it exactly as it happened.

My grandfather was very ill. He had pneumonia in the days before penicillin and oxygen tanks. My grandmother had set up a cot for him in the kitchen where the big wood-burning stove made the room warm. As with all houses built at the dawn of the twentieth century, the kitchen was an added-on room at the back of the house because of the heat it generated in the summer and the danger of fire.

My grandmother's cousin had come to stay, but she had gone to bed in the upstairs bedroom facing out onto the street.

At least three doors, two halls, and a flight of stairs separated the kitchen and her bed.

My grandfather was six-foot-four and weighed over two hundred pounds. My grandmother was five-foot-six and weighed probably a hundred ten. Hour after hour, she sat beside his bed while he slept. His breath was ragged, rattling in his chest. She kept putting cold cloths on his head and neck to cool his fever. From time to time she rolled out hot bricks from the oven to wrap in towels and place near his feet. At last, exhausted, she put her head down on the bed by his hand. Gradually, like a dawning realization, she felt something, knew something. Fearfully, she sat up.

A man stood in the doorway of the dining room. Not really in the doorway, but beyond the doorway with the darkness all around him. His dark suit was barely distinguishable. Above his white shirt and high white collar, his features were indistinct too. Only his eyes pierced the dark.

She stared at him, stared into those eyes. She could feel the skin prickling on her arms and the hair rising on the back of her neck, but she wasn't afraid. Still as a marble statue, she waited.

He nodded like a minister delivering a benediction. Then he stepped soundlessly back. The darkness closed round him like a cloak.

When she looked down, my grandfather's eyes were open. "What's wrong?" he whispered.

Shuddering so hard her teeth clicked together, she put her hands on his face and body. He was alive. Please, God! She was terrified that he was going to die, that the man in the doorway had come for her beloved husband.

"Nothing," she said. "I just dozed off and had a dream. Go back to sleep."

Not for one moment did she think a living man had somehow come into the house. Not for one moment did she believe that she had had a dream. Yet something had stood in that doorway.

When my grandfather's eyes closed, she rose. She had to steel herself at the door. Her skin was hot and cold by turns. She was holding herself so tightly against the rising panic that she could barely walk. But she took a deep breath and stepped into the darkness.

Through the dining room and into the hall, she hurried to climb the stairs. The house was pitch black and cold. Her footsteps barely sounded on the carpeted risers. She opened the door at the top of the stairs, hurried into the hall, and then opened the bedroom door.

The cousin awakened with a start. "What's wrong?"

"Nothing," my grandmother said. "Nothing. Get dressed and come down."

Something in the tone of her voice made the cousin throw back the covers immediately. Once back in the kitchen, my grandmother set about making cocoa.

As suddenly as a clock ceasing to tick, my grandfather stopped breathing.

Seventy years ago life-saving techniques consisted of a sort of primitive artificial respiration. My grandfather was twice my grandmother's size. His arms, long and heavily muscled, sagged limply when she tried to raise them. Her cousin's help was absolutely necessary to push on his chest and pump his arms to keep his lungs expanding and contracting.

As she lifted his arms over his head and lowered them, my grandmother kept glancing at the dining room, but no one was there. She kept thinking over and over, if she hadn't awakened her cousin, she would have lost her husband. She wouldn't have had the strength to do the movements by herself. Her screams for help could never have penetrated to the front of the house.

They worked on him almost half an hour before he caught his breath and started breathing on his own again.

Later after she had made him comfortable and her cousin was drinking a fresh cup of cocoa, my grandmother carried a lamp through every room on the first floor. Every room was empty and closed up tight. No window was open even a crack. No door stood ajar.

Appalled but grateful, she knew she had received a warning.

The next night about midnight, she was on watch again. My grandfather was breathing more easily. His cough had lessened. He'd eaten something during the day and sat up for an hour. Although his fever still hadn't broken, her cousin had gone to bed because he seemed so much improved.

My grandmother heard a knock at the door. So late was the hour, she was almost afraid to answer it, but this was a country town. No one who wasn't a friend or a relative would be there.

Sure enough, one of my grandfather's many cousins stood there. He had a strange, drawn look on his face. "Something told me to come," he told my grandmother warily. He glanced around him before he crossed the room to look down on my grandfather's bed. "Is Noah all right? Something told me I'd better come over." My grandmother didn't ask what. She couldn't tell him what had happened the night before. Instead, she poured her guest a cup of coffee. Just as he put it to his lips, my grandfather stopped breathing again. This time with the cousin's strength, they were able to revive the sick man quickly.

All night long the cousin stayed, helping my grandmother nurse her patient. At dawn the fever broke. He helped her change the soaked sheets and my grandfather's drenched nightshirt. Shortly after dawn my grandfather drifted into a peaceful sleep. He began to breathe normally as his lungs began to clear. The experience clarified my grandmother's vision forever. She came to believe in a purpose for every human being. My grandfather was saved because he had more to do for his family. Together they had a life to build.

Her tale instructed me. I knew without a doubt that my grandmother was not telling stories or ghost tales to scare children around a fireside. She was telling the truth. I was her granddaughter. Such a thing would happen to me.

Years passed. My grandmother died. I was completely occupied with my six-month-old daughter and was not by her side. A few years later we got the call that her cousin was very low. Very low indeed. We must come immediately. Mother and I planned to start for Arkansas the next morning.

That night, voices awoke me out of a deep sleep. They were not the voices of a dream. I opened my eyes in darkness. Nothing to see, but the voices continued. One was my grandmother's voice. She was happy. She was delighted. She was welcoming her cousin.

Their voices sounded as if they were outside the window of the room where we had been put to bed as children. Spreading a quilt or drawing up lawn chairs, the two women would sit in the darkness, talking for hours, as close as cousins, closer than best friends, dearer than sisters who saw each other only occasionally yet still remained close. They caught up on family gossip and shared the little episodes and events in their lives.

I heard them. My grandmother was welcoming her cousin whom she hadn't had a chance to visit with in a long, long time.

The next morning I told my mother what I had heard. Before I finished, she began to weep. We comforted each other because we both knew what we'd find when we got to Fort Smith.

My aunt, my grandmother's dear cousin, had died in the night in the Arkansas hospital, and I had heard my grandmother welcome her.

Years later, my mother died, unexpectedly, on the night of my birthday. I was laughing and dancing and drinking champagne in the Adolphus Hotel in Dallas while my mother collapsed in her chair in front of the television while watching the World Series. Her supper was half eaten. Her death had been a complete surprise for her too.

I flew home with my ten-year-old daughter beside me. I went into my mother's house, but she wasn't there. I sat alone in the darkness waiting for her to come. Waiting for my grandmother to reassure me that my mother was with her. But no one came.

It was the most profound disappointment of my life. Why wasn't she here? Why hadn't she at least waited in some way for me? Grief-stricken, I took her back to bury her beside her mother and father in the cemetery under the same cedar trees, now a hundred fifty years old.

I went back to my home in Dallas. A week passed. I woke in the middle of the night. I was confused. My mother was alive. I had dreamed her death. She was waiting for me to call her. Without a thought to the time, I dialed her number and waited while the phone rang and rang and rang in the empty house.

The next night I woke again. And the next.

Each time, I would dial. The phone would ring. No one would answer. I was making myself ill, trying to work during the day, waking at night, and dialing the phone.

Finally, two months later, at Christmas time, I reached for the phone but stopped myself before I dialed. I lay back in the bed with my eyes open, staring into the darkness.

She was there. I could feel her. I could almost hear her breathing. I swear I heard the rustle of her clothing. My skin tingled as I waited for the touch of her hand. The tangible never happened, but she was there. I could feel the reassurance. The love. Above all, the love. I gave myself up to it and fell immediately to sleep.

What is my assurance today? My certainty is that they are waiting for me. The circle will never be broken. They'll welcome me and we'll talk together again in the Arkansas hills.

Mona D. Sizer is no stranger to paranormal phenomena. For her first nonfiction book, *The King Ranch Story, Truth and Myth*, she researched the mysterious sensory experiences of the inhabitants of the fabulous ranch over its 150 years in the lonely brush country north of the Rio Grande. Just two of her several haunted encounters are revealed in her story "The Hills Are with Me Always." The tales of the paranormal that have come down to her regarding the Battle of Shiloh, where her great-great-grandfather was killed at Bloody Pond, are part of family legend. She used them in her novel *Angel's Caress*, written as Deana James. Mona firmly believes that not only is she a product of her past, but she carries it with her always. She is a working writer whose credits include twenty-nine books of fiction and nonfiction, three screenplays, and numerous short stories, articles, and poems, for which she has won many awards and considerable recognition. Her next book, scheduled for release in 2004, is *Texas Bandits: Real to Reel,* a serious look at the lives of infamous robbers and cutthroats in contrast with their romantic portrayals on the screen.

Photo credit: Jerry Forcher

Green Mountain State Spirits

Susan Green

Three centuries are just a blip on the radar of Earth's long history. But in this corner of New England, the year 1692 doesn't seem so terribly long ago. That's when Susannah Martin was condemned for "sundry acts of witchcraft" at the infamous Salem trials and hanged along with four others convicted of practicing the black arts. Twenty people in all were declared guilty during that time, as madness overtook the superstitious Puritans of Massachusetts.

Vermont could later lay claim to a distant echo of that shameful legacy. Among Susannah Martin's descendants was a family with the same last name that owned a Plainfield agricultural estate, which became the site of Goddard College in the late 1930s. The exposed timbers inside one of the buildings on campus came from the seventeenth-century Salem Meeting House where she was sentenced to the gallows.

It is impossible not to admire Martin, a widow from nearby Ipswich, after reading the court transcript in a 1995 book. The magistrate, John Hathorne, asked her opinion about what was then thought to be the supernaturally induced hysteria of local adolescent girls. She replied: "I do not desire to spend my judgment upon it."

"Do you think they are bewitched?" Hathorne continued, according to the official record that appears in *A Delusion of Satan* by Frances Hill.

"No, I do not think they are," Martin insisted, pointing out a biblical story about Satan posing as the ghost of the prophet Samuel. "If the devil can appear in the shape of Samuel, a glorified saint, he can appear in anyone's shape."

Ignoring that wisdom, Hathorne next demanded to know if she believed the girls were telling the truth. "They may lie for aught I know," Martin said.

"May not you lie?" he thundered.

"I dare not tell a lie if it would save my life," she pledged.

"Then you will speak the truth," the prosecutor suggested, probably anticipating a confession.

Martin responded with simple dignity: "I have spoke nothing else."

I was unaware of her existence in the 1960s while attending Goddard. The school was situated on land that once belonged to Willard and Maud Martin, who dubbed it Greatwood Farm in 1908. There, they milked shorthorn cattle, kept fancy harness horses, and raised prize sheep, while also training dogs to herd them. A perfectly bucolic enterprise, yet even six decades later strange things were still happening there.

Martin Manor, the turn-of-the-twentieth-century Georgian Revival dorm where I lodged for four or five semesters, certainly appeared to be haunted. Legend had it that the frequent creaking sounds, slamming doors, and footsteps in the hall when no living thing was nearby could be attributed to the

Manor ghost, a butler from yesteryear who had committed suicide.

One autumn day, I gathered with a group of other students — Mike, Sally, Tony, and Alice — in one of the Manor's downstairs lounges to try out the new Ouija board I'd purchased during the summer break. Sally volunteered to venture into the unknown with me that late afternoon in October. When we placed our fingertips on the heart-shaped plastic planchette, it immediately began to sail across the board, stopping too briefly on various letters for us to decipher any potential message.

With a skeptical smile, Mike started jotting down words he doubted were actually coming from the Manor's supposed spirits. "'I am dead,'" he reported. "It keeps saying that."

"How did you die?" I asked the air above my head.

"'Of drink.'" Mike dutifully translated the invisible specter's spelling into spoken language.

"Are you actually in this room?" Sally wanted to know.

"'One could speak of my presence here,'" came the reply.

"Are you a poet?" I inquired, since his or her answers were unusually lyrical.

"'Thus my bliss.'" Mike's voice was beginning to sound less contemporary and more otherworldly.

Sally was clearly unnerved. "Are you the ghost of Martin Manor?"

"'Thus my eternity.'"

Although some people suspect Ouija boards tap the unconscious mind, this complex response was far beyond the intellectual abilities of the participating humans.

"What do you think of us?" It was Mike himself, now newly converted and worried that we were in some kind of danger.

"'Doomed with my soul,'" the disembodied drunken poet proclaimed, and I sensed a collective shiver running through the group. Sally and I took our hands away from the board.

"Hey, it's time for dinner," Tony suggested, glancing at his watch.

"Yeah, I'm hungry," added Alice, although she looked too rattled to hold down food.

Hesitant to insult such an articulate apparition by cutting off communication so abruptly, I put my fingers back on the planchette. "When can we contact you again?"

Before Sally could match my gesture, the Ouija began to speak once more through Mike: "'When the moon dies.'" Everyone was silent.

On the way to the dining hall, Sally and I debated what "when the moon dies" might mean. When it's on the wane? When the sun comes up? After some celestial catastrophe? As we passed by a gigantic maple, the tree suddenly came crashing down about 50 feet from us. We ran the rest of the way. And never again attempted the Ouija together.

For all of Martin Manor's mystery, an adjacent part of the campus always held even greater metaphysical allure for me. I was entranced by the Garden House, a step-gabled Tudor Revival cottage added to the estate in 1925. On one front corner of the roof, the forces of evil are kept at bay by a rather benign gargoyle in the shape of a squirrel clutching an acorn.

Within, I learned much later, were the wooden beams that Willard Martin apparently had spared no expense to obtain as a way of honoring his maligned ancestor.

Massachusetts lawmakers finally exonerated all the Salem witches in 2001. Yet I still wonder if Susannah Martin protests her cruel fate by forever roaming the Garden House — scene of many a student party in my day. Not knowing of her sad saga back then, I never tried to make contact via the Ouija board.

In 1970, however, I wound up in the Boston suburb of Danvers, once the original Salem Village. I lived on Summer Street, where a 300-year-old house just down the road had been the home of the first person the paranoid Puritans arrested: Sarah Good, who was hanged along with Susannah on that July day in 1692.

I haven't a clue what all this means. But, possibly doomed with the soul of some alcoholic bard from the Great Beyond, I wait for the moon to die.

Susan Green reviews films for *Box Office* magazine in California, and works as a freelance reporter for *Vermont Sunday Magazine* and the weekly *Seven Days*. She has won several journalism honors, including two first-place feature story awards from the New England Press Association. In 1985 she wrote *Bread & Puppet: Stories of Struggle and Faith From Central America,* a book about the Vermont-based theatrical troupe. Green contributed a chapter to *Backstory 3: Interviews with Screenwriters of the 1960s,* published by the University of California Press in 1997. One of her essays, "Madness along the Milky Way," is included in an anthology titled *The Realities of Breastfeeding: Reflections by Contemporary Women* (Bergin & Garvey, 1997). In 1998 Green co-authored the not-so-unofficial *Law & Order: The Unofficial Companion*; a second, expanded edition came out in

November 1999 (Renaissance Books/St. Martin Press). Her short fiction has been published in small literary journals: *96 Inc* (Boston, Massachusetts), *The Villager* (Bronxville, New York), *Hidden Manna* (Houston, Texas), *Vermont Ink*, and *Out of Line* (Henderson, Kentucky).

A Lighted Fog

Anika Logan

My friend Shayna and I went out for coffee that Wednesday evening. It was just another ordinary night, nothing special. On our way home we came over the hill and passed our old high school standing a hundred feet or so back from the road. Stopping briefly to glance at it, we both commented how different it looked under the shroud of darkness — eerie, and almost gloomy. I imagined the empty hallways and the rows of lockers, not to mention the classrooms standing vacant, just waiting until morning to be filled with the raucous laughter and conversations of its occupants. We hadn't been students there in almost nine years. It seemed like such a long time since I'd had the concerns of a teenager, a lifetime really.

After dropping me off at my basement apartment, Shayna headed home in the opposite direction and I prepared to go to bed. It had been a busy day at work and I was tired and ready for a good night's sleep. Making sure the lock on my front door was firmly in place, I turned off the lights and went into my bedroom. My cat, Arthur, a beautiful striped tabby, followed me in and after a few minutes of rubbing against me, I patted his head and gave him his goodnight hug, and then he cuddled up on the end of my bed as he always does. I shut my bedroom door, turned off the light, and crawled between my covers.

Although I live alone in a relatively small apartment, I always feel safer with my door shut at night. I'm not exactly sure why that is, fear of fire perhaps. Arthur doesn't seem to mind at all. Even before I started closing my door at night, Arthur slept on my bed with me and hardly made a peep until he heard me rousing in the morning.

I fell into a deep sleep very quickly that night and slept soundly until something woke me quite unexpectedly. I opened my eyes and lay there for a few seconds, listening to see if I could identify what had awakened me. All was still in my apartment. My heart sped up and I felt a cold chill run down my spine as my mind began to envision all sorts of heinous scenarios. Raising my head off my pillow I looked at the clock to my right and saw the time in big red numbers — 2:36 A.M.

As I sat up, I noticed that Arthur was no longer on the end of my bed. Strange, I thought. This got me to worrying and I realized that whatever had woken me up was not in my imagination or part of a dream, as Arthur had been awakened as well. I grabbed my robe off a nearby chair and pulled it on. It was then that I noticed the fog. My bedroom door was wide open and there sat Arthur just inside my bedroom, in the frame of it really, just sitting there staring out into the hallway, staring out at — what I really couldn't say for sure.

With my heart almost beating out of my chest, I inched closer to the doorway, attempting to be as quiet as possible so as not to startle my cat — and disturb whatever was brewing in my hallway. I needn't have worried — Arthur seemed not to even notice my approach, so intent was he on the happenings just outside the doorway.

I stood a few inches behind my cat's still body, just staring myself and watching something I had never seen before. I was frightened in one sense because I didn't understand, but I was fascinated in another because I doubted that this was something I might ever experience again, right in front of my own eyes, in my own small basement apartment.

Trying to make sense of it in my own head was difficult. It seemed almost to be a type of fog swirling about in a gentle, airy sort of way. I was too nervous to approach it any closer or to reach my hands out to see if it resembled the dew of a spring morning or was like the dampness of fog or even the soft, wet quality of a light snowfall.

There seemed to be a degree of light shining through it as well. Not a strong florescent light but more like the fading light at the end of a day as the sun dips beneath the Earth, setting in the west for its good-night rest. It wasn't luminescent but a kind and welcoming light — warm, comforting — but also I couldn't help feeling a degree of sadness observing it from where I stood. That was the word that came to my mind all of a sudden as I watched and took it all in — sadness.

Arthur sat mesmerized and soundless, not uttering a cry or a meow or any other cat sound. I was speechless, spellbound, and we both remained rooted to the spot, our eyes glued to the apparition of lighted fog that hung in my hallway. I really have no idea how much time passed. It could have been a few seconds, a few minutes, or even a half an hour. Finally I began to feel cold and yearned for the warmth of my bed. With the lighted fog still there, I called Arthur's name once and told him we should go back to bed. He didn't move or look up at me; he just continued to stare into the fog. I said his name once more, a little louder this time, and he turned his head and looked at me. Smiling, I told him he'd seen enough and that we were going to go back to sleep.

With one final look in the fog's direction, I shook my head in disbelief, picked Arthur up (he didn't protest one bit), closed my bedroom door, and went back to bed. It took him a few minutes but finally Arthur drifted back to sleep, only this time he was snuggled up as close as he could get on my left side. Sleep didn't come as easily for me this time. My mind was churning with speculation as to what I'd just witnessed. The questions abounded. Questions, of course, that did not come with their own set of answers. I tossed and turned but finally my body and mind allowed me to rest.

When I woke in the morning, I was afraid to look towards my bedroom door for fear that it would be standing open and the fog, complete with its own unique light, would still be there. It wasn't. Opening my door tentatively, I peered out into the hallway. Everything looked as normal as it always did. To look at it under the scrutiny of morning you would never think anything at all out of the ordinary had transpired the night before. But of course, I knew better. Something had happened last night, and Arthur and I had both seen it. Out of the ordinary or extraordinary, however you choose to think of it.

I went about my everyday morning routine, made sure Arthur had enough food and water for the day, and headed off to work. All morning I tried my best to do everything I could to keep my mind off what had happened in my apartment the previous night. What exactly had taken place? I asked myself. And why in my home of all places? I did not have a clue and I was afraid to tell a soul for fear they would think that I had gone totally crazy.

I was just getting ready to leave my office for lunch when my sister called.

"Did you hear what happened last night?" she asked me.

"No," I answered. "I didn't get the chance to listen to the news this morning."

"I don't think it's made the news yet, Anika. It's local."

I was afraid to ask but of course I had to. "What happened, Lindy?" My voice had dropped an octave or two.

"A grade ten student, a girl, was murdered last night. Apparently she was beaten, then her throat was slit and she was thrown off the roof of the high school, if you can believe it! Some students on the first floor saw her body lying sprawled out on the field during class. Isn't that horrible?! Can you believe what this world is coming to?! In our own community!"

"Oh my God!" I shrieked. "Oh my God — the poor girl! Murdered! And practically in our own backyard! How she must have suffered those last few moments of her life!"

I know, it's incomprehensible. The police have not released her name yet. But I heard through the grapevine that —"

The events in my apartment came sharply back into focus. I cut my sister off with a question of my own. "Lindy, does anyone have any idea around what time she was killed during the night? I mean, was it early in the evening or later that night because Shayna and I drove by the high school around, let's see, sometime shortly after ten."

"No, it was later than that. The word is it was sometime around 2:30 in the morning."

I froze at her words. 2:30 A.M. I had been awakened quite suddenly at around 2:36 A.M. The light, the fog — it all made sense. A life was being taken at that moment, a young high school girl, her life just beginning.

"Anika? Anika, are you still there? Are you listening to me? Hello?"

I wasn't listening anymore. The lighted fog. Arthur standing in my doorway mesmerized by it. 2:30 A.M. I could think of nothing else.

Anika Logan is a freelance writer of poetry, short stories, personal essays, and articles on writing. Her work has appeared widely over the Internet, including at Widethinker, Absolutewrite, The Sidewalk's End, Seedfusion, LIA Magazine, Everywriter, and Donard Publishing. Anika is an animal lover, and plays tennis, practices yoga, and admits to being a voracious reader. She resides in Eastern Canada where she is, as always, busy at work on her latest project. More information about Anika's works can be found at her web site — www.authorsden.com/anikalogan. She can be reached via e-mail at ani_logan@yahoo.com.

When Souls Go Thirsty

Swapna Goel

"Never sleep thirsty. Never!" As my head touches the pillow, Mom's words ring in my mind. But I am too upset to make a trip to the kitchen for the water jug. The smell of death still fills the house, emptied of its most important member. My tired eyelids droop but I know sleep will provide no respite. Scenes from the morning funeral replay in my mind like an endless reel of film. I swallow. My throat is parched and my eyes are watery. Mom never forgot to keep two glasses of water at my bedside, and now she's gone. Dead.

She knew this would happen. Only we did not believe her. At the hospital yesterday, Mom refused to take her eyes off Papa, waving aside whomever stood in between. "Let me see him, I'm going."

She believed in the voices she heard. She lived by them. The same voice had told her soon she was to fall into a deep sleep.

We never heard these so-called voices, and were skeptical.

Papa and my sis laughed. They reminded her it was a simple biopsy. Mom would be out of the operation theatre in less than an hour, well in time to have lunch with us. She just shook her head and continued to hold Dad's gaze.

Two hours later her surgeon emerged from the theatre and three pairs of eyes locked onto him.

"Not mmm... malignant, I hope?" my dad stammered.

"I did not take out her lump. I doubt it's malignant," the doctor replied.

You could hear us exhale.

"But," the surgeon put a hand on Papa's shoulder, "something unexpected happened. Even before the biopsy, she suffered a cardiac arrest and slipped into coma."

"Impossible! She was never a heart patient," I cried.

Dad stared back at the doctor, his eyes wild.

The surgeon threw up his hands. "Such things happen. We're at a loss to explain."

Mom's words echo in all our minds: "I'm going. I'll fall into a deep sleep. I know."

That instant I begin to believe in those voices.

The same day I start hearing them.

"Drink water." The words boom in my head. I choose to ignore; they grow louder. Terrified, I gulp down a glassful.

Mother once told us, "Thirsty souls wander in the night. They may get lost and find it difficult to re-enter their bodies before sunlight." Parents often scare little children into doing things with such stories. I never thought she was serious, though I dutifully drank the water she got for me.

It had been a bad day. By the end of it, I put it all down to fancy. I flop on the bed and shut my eyes. I hear it again. It starts as a whisper, "Water!" I move not a muscle. After a while the call gets more insistent. "Water. Water. Water." It beats on me. It drives me mad.

I look on the bedside table. No water jug. I check the dresser. Not there either. Thirsty, I move out of my room. I'm in the study amid the bookshelves. The voice is now a chant. Still can't find the damn water. Deafened, I glide out.

My sister lets out a snore. I've reached her room. I throw open the window as my restlessness grows. "Water!" The shriek is too loud to bear. Just then my eyes drift to a half-empty glass standing beside the bed. I guzzle down 'til the last drop. I want more.

I reach out. It's the balcony. I must look further.

Something blinds me. I twist in pain. Who shakes me? My eyes fly open. I see Papa bending over me with a wet napkin.

"You okay, Pet?" he asks.

I feel drained, but manage to nod.

"Thank God! I checked on you last night. You looked ghastly."

Papa's words make no sense, though I sure feel unusual.

"Whole night I sat here, sponging your burning forehead and praying as you tossed in pain," he continued.

Strange. I remember nothing.

My sister runs in just then. "Someone was in my room last night, Papa. My window is open. I'm sure I shut it last night."

Dad tells her she must have made a mistake. She is too excited to listen.

"I checked my room, all was the same. Then I went to the balcony. Guess what I found there? My glass. But I'd left it near my bed last night after a drink. How did it get past the locked balcony door?" Breathless, she then drags Dad away to show.

My head reels as I hear her story. I remember going to her room. I clearly remember drinking the water. No, it was not a dream. The scene is etched vividly in my mind. But didn't Papa just mention I'd been too sick to move last night? And he spent the entire night next to me?

Can a person be in two places at one time?

If I was in my room, who had been in the balcony?

Was Ma right about wandering souls?

I don't have the ghost of an answer.

However, I know one thing: Next time I hear the voice, I will do as it says.

 Swapna Goel was a journalist who was shocked to discover she enjoyed creating fiction more than reporting facts. Now a storyteller, she lives in India but has been published widely both home and abroad. Her fiction, humorous essays, and memoirs have appeared in many leading print and online publications. She tries not to get tied to any genre and writes across the board on any topic that catches her fancy. Her next work to hit the shelves is a friendship story to be published by Conari/Red Wheel/Weiser in the fall of 2003. Swapna believes, "Till I got life, I got a story left to tell."

The Play Date

Silvana Soleri

Our second-floor flat had windows that faced three directions — east, south, and west. While the twelve hours of uninterrupted daylight would have been enough of a feature to distinguish it from similar flats, there were others. The small apartment house was on a block at the end of a street that was disconnected from its main artery by an intersecting road. No children lived on that peculiar stretch of road, except for me. The typical sounds of a residential street were absent. There was no laughter, no crying, no playing. To describe it merely as quiet would be an understatement — it was beyond quiet. This neighborhood was silent. This was the kind of silence found only in desolate places — a mystical, penetrating silence that was fertile ground for the paranormal. Here was a silence so palpable it would rumble in my ears like a passing freight train.

Across the street, stood a nineteenth-century church with a small cemetery in back. Its huge bells tolled at nine, noon, and five, and were the only predictable break in the eerie quietude. Except on rare occasions when someone would drop by for a visit, my days were spent alone in my grandmother's care. From that perspective, everyday life droned on in a seamless continuum.

These circumstances led me to become skilled at entertaining myself, and so I relied heavily on my creativity to fill in the gaps. My grandmother's bedroom lent itself well to this — it was rife with possibilities for a bored little girl. It was large and sunny, with polished hardwood floors that were great for dancing and skidding across in my socks. In this room was a mirrored cherry vanity table that was a favorite prop for many of my productions. It had a central mirror, with two smaller, hinged mirrors flanking it on both sides. The entire entryway of the bedroom could be seen in the reflection.

One day, while playing at the mirror, I became aware that someone had entered the room and was standing behind me. Although I was looking directly in the mirror, I did not see anyone in its reflection. I turned around, expecting to see a family member or some other recognizable face. Instead, I found myself looking straight into the face of a complete stranger. I gasped and jerked back a little.

Standing eyeball to eyeball with me was a little girl, exactly my height and approximately my age. I assumed she was there visiting with her parents and was sent in to play with me.

"Hi," I said. She did not respond. She did not smile. She did not even move very much. She only stared deeply into my eyes, clutching a small bouquet of flowers.

This, to me, seemed a strange interaction that required closer scrutiny. As I stepped around to her side, she followed me with her gaze. As I observed her more carefully, I realized that her manner of dress was strange as well. She wore a long, white cotton gown, with a matching bonnet and laced-up boots. Her cheeks were rosy red, her eyes round and dark. I waited for her to say something or do something, but she did neither. She just stared, so I gave it another try.

"What's your name?" I asked. Again no answer. I thought that if she was there to play, and there was no reason to believe otherwise, we ought to get on with it. Besides, I considered this visit a stroke of luck, and was not about to waste the opportunity. With this in mind, I took the initiative to resume playing, assuming she would join me. Not more than a few seconds had passed before I looked up again, and saw that she had disappeared.

Without a sound or a trace, she had vanished as mysteriously as she had appeared. I wondered who this girl was and how she got there. My eyes moved to the doorway that led out of the bedroom into the living room.

As I peered out, I could see the sofa and chairs just sitting there, vacant. If we had guests, that is where they would be. Sensing that something was not quite right, I went to the kitchen. My grandmother was in there, going about her ironing. I thought surely she would have some explanation for what had just happened. Maybe she could even get the girl to come back and play with me.

"Who was just here, Nana?"

"No one. Why, dear?"

"Nobody?" I thought perhaps I didn't make myself clear. "Who was the little girl that came in the bedroom, Nana?"

"What little girl? Nobody came over. I didn't let anybody in the door."

"I don't know where she came from, she was just standing there."

"Who was she? What did she look like?"

"She was wearing a long, long white dress and a hat."

"What? Show me this little girl."

"I can't, Nana. She's gone now." This was not going at all as I had hoped.

"Gone, huh? So, what did she want, anyway?"

"Nothing."

"Nothing? That's a little strange. She must have said something to you."

"No, Nana, she wouldn't talk. Can't we go find her and bring her back here?"

"Well, if she won't talk, we can't really do that. Besides, it's getting late, maybe you should go find something else to do."

With that, I went back to the bedroom, hoping that the little girl would come back. In fact, I went on hoping for days afterward, but she never did return.

This incident took place in the early sixties. As conventional wisdom of the times would have it, the little girl was just a product of an active imagination — except for a couple of important facts. Although I was only five years old at the time, I remember the experience in full detail, as vividly now as then. Also, since my family had only recently emigrated from Europe, they spoke little English. Consequently, my childhood was insulated — we did not engage in activities that featured such things as historical costumes. Not even television programming in those days was as sophisticated as it is now. Therefore, up to that point, I had never been exposed to clothing like that before. I simply could not have imagined something I had never seen.

Silvana Soleri is a freelance writer living in Florida. Her personal writing is in the creative nonfiction and essay genres. Often though, she can be found hard at work on various copywriting projects.

Now I'm a Believer

Elizabeth L. Blair

As a flight attendant, I have stayed in my share of hotels. Some of the hotels I have had the pleasure of sleeping in have rumors of apparitions of ladies roaming the halls and the unexplained scent of roses filling some rooms. At one hotel I stayed in, it was said that hotel guests have been seen staying in the lobby out of refusal to stay in the guestrooms a moment longer because of odd occurrences. The stories are endless. Personally, I had not experienced anything supernatural other than strange dreams during my stays at many of these hotels. Honestly, I wasn't sure the stories had any merit, until one day when my turn came.

I remember the day clearly: It was a Friday in November. My crew was scheduled to stay at an old hotel in Louisville that had rumors of strange occurrences. The tales didn't cross my mind when I saw where my overnight was to be. After all, the stories were just rumors. Basically, that's what I attribute the stories — just rumors. This particular trip I was flying with two flight attendants, Bob and Anne. We enjoyed each other's company and had been having a great trip. When we arrived at the historical hotel we all agreed to meet for dinner in the hotel's restaurant. We talked, laughed, and had a grand time. Halfway through dinner we heard the beautiful voice of a woman singing in the cocktail lounge. We all decided to stop in and listen to her for a while once dinner was through. We were not in the lounge for more than a half-hour when the yawns began and we all decided to return to our rooms. All three of us were on different floors, so one by one we stepped off the elevator. "Goodnight, see you in the morning," we all said. We had ten hours before having to report for work, more than enough time to get a good night's sleep. Well, some of us.

I slept through most of the night with the exception of someone knocking on my door about 2 A.M. When I groggily looked through the peephole, no one was there. At three o'clock, I awoke to another knock. I climbed out of bed to find no one there, again. I assumed it was another mistake and crawled back into bed until my travel alarm sounded three hours later, forcing me out of bed for good. I took a long, hot shower. When I was through I stepped out of the shower and on to the white bath mat. I wrapped myself in the hotel's white fluffy towels and walked into the bedroom. As soon as I walked into the room, I stopped. There was music playing. I looked to the corner of the room the music was coming from and saw that the radio was on.

"That's strange," I thought. I never turn the radio on in hotels. I rely on my personal alarm clock and a backup wake-up call from the front desk, so I knew I didn't set the alarm. I came to the conclusion that the person who stayed in the room before me must have set the alarm. I pushed the alarm button off, but nothing happened. I looked on the side of the radio to find the radio switch was in the on position. Still not convinced, I pushed the alarm button to see what time it was set for. Assuming I would see 6 A.M., I was surprised to see it set for three in the afternoon. There I stood staring at the radio as it played a blues song I was unfamiliar with. Someone turned it on, and it wasn't me. I froze. Standing there dripping wet with a towel on my head and a towel around me, my heart began to pound and my breathing was getting heavy. I didn't know what to do. I glanced at the closed closet door. Was someone in there? I looked at the latch on the door that led to the hall. The double latch and chain were both still locked and there were no adjoining doors. No one could have entered my room. Nervously, I tiptoed over to the door of the closet. I opened it quickly and jumped back, expecting to see someone. No one was there. My uniform was hanging in place just where I had left it. I breathed a sigh of relief. Then panic overcame me again. "The bed!" I thought. "Was someone under it all night?" I dropped to my knees and looked underneath — nothing. I let out another sigh. "I am being ridiculous," I thought, my heart still pounding. I quickly dressed, packed, and left my room. On my ride down the elevator I swore I wouldn't tell anyone about my stay. No one would believe me anyway.

When I arrived downstairs in the lobby, both of my crewmembers were already waiting for me. We still had twenty minutes before the airport shuttle was scheduled to depart. "What are you both doing down here so early?" I asked as I approached them. I saw they both looked exhausted with dark circles under their eyes. Anne's hair was normally in a cute style, but it wasn't today. In fact, it looked wet.

"Let's just say neither of us slept," Anne stated.

Bob chimed in, "Yeah, you know those stories about this hotel? Well, let's just say they're not rumors."

My eyes grew big as I asked, "Why? What happened?"

"All crazy kinds of things. I don't know where to start. My faucet was turning on and off all by itself and I heard creaking in my room as if someone was walking. I even felt my bed move as if someone sat down on it. I woke up scared to death," Anne rambled. "I was so frightened that I took a shower, dressed, and left. I've been down here for a while, putting on my makeup," she said, lifting the makeup bag she was holding.

I looked at Bob. "What happened to you?" I asked.

"Someone kept knocking on my door, and every time I answered it there was no one there. When I finished taking a shower, I heard a noise in the bedroom, and when I walked in the TV was on," he said convincingly.

My stomach turned. "Are you sure?"

"I never turn on the TV in the morning; there's nothing on." I believed him. Bob continued, "You must think we're both crazy. You look like you got a great night's sleep."

I was faced with admitting what I experienced or denying everything. But, finding it so odd that all three of us had strange encounters, I started, "Actually, I did sleep well. But I had a couple of knocks on my door last night, too. But no one was there. I thought they were mistakes." The pair knew exactly what I was talking about, so I continued with the odd radio occurrence. "I thought I was losing it," I finished.

"No, it was not your imagination," they both said in unison.

Just then, a smiling janitor walked by pushing an oversized broom. In a southern accent he said, "Hey, kids, did y'all have a good night?"

The three of us half-heartedly nodded. The man caught on to our weariness and said, "Oh, you had visitors last night, didn't ya? Made believers out of you, huh? Well, you ain't the first and you ain't the last." He chuckled and kept on walking.

Elizabeth Blair is the author of many published works found in a variety of anthologies and online publications. With both ink and jet fuel in her blood, she lives her life as both a freelance writer and flight attendant in Tucson, Arizona, with her wonderful husband, Jeff, and two stepsons. Currently, she is working on her first book, a compilation of stories about her humorous, emotional, and lively journey in the airline industry. She can be e-mailed at elblair99@yahoo.com.

Friendly Ghosts

Valerie Dansereau

After months of hunting for a multi-family property, my husband and I finally found our dream home. It was a huge Victorian, built by a New Bedford whaling captain in 1863, but had been converted to a four-family home. The cellar door had a painted skull and crossbones and an ominous message: "THIS BASEMENT IS HAUNTED!" We ignored the message. It was a dirt cellar, and in one corner was a huge mountain of dirt that looked like something Edgar Allen Poe would write about.

Within twenty-four hours of moving in, the first incidents began to happen. The kitchen faucet would spontaneously turn on and off. My watch disappeared. Although I'm not the most organized person in the world, I always put my watch in the same place. "I'm sure the baby just ran off with it," my husband reassured me. "It'll turn up."

It did turn up, in a way and time that made me realize that something very odd was going on in this house. It was 5 A.M. and I was the first to rise, as was my routine. I went to take a shower in the dark, silent house, and when I returned to my bedroom, there was my watch in the middle of the bedroom floor. It had not been there ten minutes earlier.

There was no one else awake in the house.

Our keys began disappearing at frequent intervals, and although we recognized that sometimes it was due to absent-mindedness on our part, the frequency of the disappearances was out of the ordinary. On one particular occasion, my husband's set of keys disappeared. We searched high and low, somewhat frantically retracing his steps. The keys suddenly appeared on top of the toolbox on his truck. What made this unsettling was that Dennis had opened the toolbox several times to see if the keys had fallen inside. How could they suddenly be on top of a toolbox that had been repeatedly opened?

A few weeks after we moved in, around 3 A.M., my husband left our bed for a couple of minutes, came back, and whispered in my ear, "I could swear I just saw a dude going through our closet."

"Sure, Dennis," I murmured, still more asleep than awake. I was sure he was also half asleep, or that there had been some trick of the light.

The very next night, after everyone was in bed, I came into the bedroom and saw a man looking intently in the closet, just as Dennis had described him. He was rummaging frantically, and seemed very disturbed at not finding what he was looking for. He was wearing a brown business suit, and was very tall, around 6'3"? or so. His shoulders were broad and his legs were thin as twigs, appearing too thin to hold the solidness of his upper body. No sooner had I focused on this image than it was gone.

A few days later as I was making dinner, I strode across the kitchen and was about to open the refrigerator, when there at the side of the fridge stood the same man. We were face to face, so close I could see the worry-worn creases on his face, so close I could read the expression in his eyes. It was a pleading look, as if he wanted something from me. I was startled, but not frightened by his appearance, and didn't feel in any way threatened by him. Again, once I was able to focus, he disappeared.

There was only one incident that made me wonder if there was a degree of danger from our ghosts. We had come to believe there was more than one ghost, as we could often hear a baby crying. In fact, one of our tenants has also heard the baby crying. My younger daughter was barely over a year old when an odd thing occurred. She was standing in front of the front door looking up, as if at a child slightly bigger than she was. "Rebecca, what are you looking at?" I asked softly. She continued to stare at whatever she saw that I did not, when suddenly she rose about a foot off the ground as if someone had picked her up, and then was tossed backward against the hallway wall. She ran to me crying, and for the first time I felt a degree of uneasiness about our spiritual company.

A friend of mine had some time on her hands and began doing some research on my house. She learned some details about the whaling captain who had built the house, including that he had been married three times and had three children. She provided me with his picture and his obituary. I was disappointed to realize that this was not the man I had seen.

However, knowing his name and his background, my husband and I were able to find his grave in a neighborhood cemetery. To our astonishment, all three of his children died by the age of nine. Two died as babies.

The longer we have lived here, the less often we see the ghost. For a period of time, both my husband and I would see his shadow sitting in the recliner in the middle of the night, but as time passed, the sightings became less frequent. We wonder if it requires some special energy on his part to make himself visible.

More often now, there are only occasional attention-getting tactics that let us know we are not alone. Frequently our closet door will swing open and closed for several minutes at a time. Recently in late summer, our air conditioner inexplicably turned itself on.

There were two other semi-disturbing incidents. One of the upstairs apartments became vacant, and my husband was doing improvements when suddenly the bedroom door shut and he couldn't get it open for quite a while. Another time we had a minor fire in our kitchen, and while Dennis and I were examining what was damaged, the Crockpot suddenly hurled itself to the floor between us.

For the most part, we feel we can coexist happily with our ghosts. It adds charm to our home not knowing for sure what may happen next.

Valerie Dansereau grew up in the small southwestern Massachusetts town of Middleboro. She graduated from Babson School for Financial Studies in 2001, and attends Bristol Community College, majoring in Business Management. She has dabbled in writing all her life and has also been published in *True Confessions*. The incident described in "Friendly Ghost" is not the first supernatural encounter she has had. There have been other sightings of light and sensations of presences, but this was the first time a ghost took human form. Her interest in psychic experiences began with her own mother's gift of ESP. She has always been fascinated with astrology, the tarot, and mediums. She lives in New Bedford, Massachusetts, with her husband, Dennis, and two daughters, Bethany, 18, and Rebecca, 4. She enjoys the outdoors, particularly camping and gardening, and loves being with children. She values family above all else.

Historic Haunted Forts

Docia Williams

In 1995, while researching my West Texas book, *Phantoms of the Plains*, my husband, Roy Williams, and I stopped at historic Fort Leaton near the far West Texas town of Presidio. We were accompanied on our visit to the fort by the friendly park ranger on duty, Vivano Garcia. I told Mr. Garcia that I was interested in ghost stories of the region and asked him if there were any stories attached to the former fort. He said there were a couple of rooms where psychics had felt presences, and added that he would like to see if I could pick up any "vibes." He didn't volunteer much more information. As we strolled through the sprawling fort, I suddenly felt very cold, and I had a prickly, goose-bumpy sensation in my arms. I asked Mr. Garcia if the room we were in was one of those where "something" might be. He answered that he had heard that one of the early owners, a member of the Burgess family, had been shot in that room by the sheriff. Still, in another room, a rather dark place where only slit-like windows high up on the walls near the ceiling admitted a bit of light, I had the same uncomfortable feeling, accompanied by a feeling of deep sadness. Again, I asked our host if something had happened in that room as well. He said yes, that room was where Mr. Leaton, the last owner of the hacienda-fort, described as an "evil" man, kept his servants confined whenever he deemed them guilty of an infraction. Some were incarcerated there for very long periods of time, thus the feeling of melancholy I felt in that room. I do not even pretend to be psychic, but I had really strong feelings in that old fort, and I was relieved when our visit came to an end.

During that same trip to West Texas, we stopped for a couple of hours at Fort Clark Springs. A friend of mine had lived there until recently when she moved back to San Antonio. Her house, a former set of officer's quarters at the old Indian fort, was up for sale. She gave us a key and asked us to check to see if everything was in order, and that no shingles had blown off the roof during a recent storm.

When we went in, we were assailed by the smell of bacon cooking and coffee boiling. My friend, Barbara Niemann, had told us that she had often been awakened by the aromas of coffee and bacon, even though neither she nor her husband drank coffee, and they very seldom cooked bacon! When we got into the kitchen, of course, the stove was cold, nothing was cooking, and the aroma slowly disappeared.

We spoke with several occupants of the old quarters along Colony Row, many of whom experience the smell of coffee and bacon cooking early in the morning. We learned in the old days, when the fort was occupied by the U.S. Cavalry, that the officers were assigned "strikers." These were young enlisted personnel who would come in early before the officers and their families arose, strike up the woodstove (that's where the expression "striker" originated), and start the breakfast preparations. They would boil a pot of coffee (there were no percolators in the 1880s!) and fry a skillet of bacon. It is quite evident some of these early soldiers are still attached to their old jobs, or maybe they are just hungry. But we both smelled that bacon frying, and even my husband, an avowed agnostic when it comes to ghosts, agrees that "something" is still cooking at old Fort Clark!

On one of my "Spirits of San Antonio" ghost tours, which I do around San Antonio from time to time, I had an eerie experience. I was not alone when this happened. There were several witnesses. We visited a lovely old house, known to be haunted, over on Cedar Street in San Antonio's historic King William District. It had recently been converted into a bed and breakfast inn. The owner of the house was Betty Gatlin, an attractive widow. When four or five of our group went into a bedroom, one of the ladies exclaimed to our hostess what a charming dried arrangement of flowers she had on the bedroom dresser. She asked Betty how she had arranged it. Betty told her to pick it up and examine it if she would like, and the lady did just that. The dried flowers had been placed in a lovely old antique brass vase. Suddenly, the whole bouquet started trembling and vibrating violently. I never saw anything like it. The lady was totally startled, and just hung on to the vase for dear life for a moment and then deposited the whole thing back on the dresser. We were all just dumbfounded! The flowers and foliage were not just trembling slightly, they were moving as if they were afflicted with severe palsy! We were all convinced that Betty's ghostly inhabitants were hard at work to make our visit memorable!

Yes, I believe there are such things as ghosts. And I am still finding them as I go about writing some of my stories about the supernatural side of San Antonio!

Docia Schultz Williams is a professional writer, lecturer, and certified professional tour guide. She makes her home in San Antonio, Texas.

She has conducted tours all over the United States and to many foreign destinations, including Europe, China, Africa, Canada, and South America. She resided for a number of years in both England and Spain where she pursued her interest in the arts, history, and antiques. She is a member of the Professional Tour Guides Association of San Antonio.

Co-author of the book, *Spirits of San Antonio and South Texas*, she is also the author of *Ghosts Along the Texas Coast*, *Phantoms of the Plains*, *When Darkness Falls*, *Best Tales of Texas Ghosts*, *The History and Mystery of the Menger Hotel*, and *Exploring San Antonio with Children, A Guide for Family Activities*. She originated a nighttime tour, "Spirits of San Antonio," featuring the most haunted spots in town, which received the prestigious "Gemmy" award from the Midwest Travel Writers' Association for being one of the country's truly unique travel experiences. A frequent club and convention speaker, she has appeared in many Texas cities. She is also a featured cruise lecturer with the Norwegian and Commodore cruise lines. She will soon have another book ready for press, much to the delight of her readers and her publishing house.

Haunted

Charley Scholl

As I entered my bus that fateful day, I had no idea that my life was about to change forever. How many times had I driven through that back-road intersection with the almost nonexistent visibility to the right? There were large pine trees running from the ditch as far as the eye could see to the right, the evergreens thick and lush. In a car, a driver could see beneath the heavy branches and see oncoming traffic, but in a large commercial vehicle such as a bus or dump truck, the driver had no such luck.

And as luck would have it that fateful October day, I made a left turn onto Robin Road. I proceeded about a half-mile and slowed to scan my mirror for riders at the only stop on that road. As I sped up, I noticed a car passing me. I looked down and realized I was only going 35 miles an hour. I got up to 40 as I watched the car enter and then clear the intersection now looming before me.

As I neared the intersection, a flash in the trees to my right caught the corner of my eye. I craned my head to look and found myself looking into the eyes of a man on a motorcycle. He was traveling at a high rate of speed and had a look of horror on his face as he realized just what was about to meet him at this particular intersection. He was not wearing a helmet, and the stop sign loomed in front of him.

I'll never forget that twisted, contorted look of horror on his face as long as I live. I've never seen a human face stretched like that ever, before or since. I literally saw his life pass before his eyes in that instant. And, believe me, this all happened in an instant. I immediately turned back and gripped the wheel hard, jamming on the brake. We slid, and slid. I found myself literally standing in my seatbelt in an effort to get just a little bit more braking effort, but it was not to be on this day. I gripped the steering wheel hard at 10 and 2 o'clock, trying to rein in my bus. I swear I would have torn that steering wheel right off had it been made of a weaker material. The fifteen or so students left on the bus took one wild ride that day. We slid for what seemed like forever on the dirt road.

And then it happened. The motorcyclist came back into view, at a high rate of speed. He was bent forward over his bike, twisting the handle grip as hard as he could to get all the speed he could get, just one more time. As he flew through the intersection, I knew he wasn't going to make it on that old bike. I realized that his decision had been to outrun the bus rather than try to stop, which would have been impossible anyway.

As he crossed in front of me, just before impact, I heard myself cry out, "OH MY GOD!" And then, a small bump. The motorcyclist's head hit the front of the bus as it made contact with the bike. Both bike and rider hit the ground and came back up. The rider was now limp and unconscious as he and the bike hit the front of the bus one more time. Then the rider sailed through the air into the left ditch, some 25 to 30 feet ahead of us. The bike slid under the bus and was dragged a few more feet by a cross member, and then we ground to a stop.

I was fine, not hurt at all, and grabbed the mike to call for help. I had to give coordinates, but my mind went blank. Mercifully, the bus had come to rest right next to the crossed road signs. I asked for the police department and an ambulance and gave the street address. I checked the kids and asked if they were okay. They all said they were as they picked themselves up off the floor. I put the bus in neutral and threw the parking brake, shutting off the engine.

Mike, who drove the route next to mine, radioed that he was a mile or two away and would come and get my kids and get them out of there. I now headed out to what I was sure would be my first encounter with a dead body. I gulped and stepped forward, grabbing my first aid kit as I left the bus. A high school student said he was coming with me. I told him he didn't have to, that the man was probably dead. He answered that he wasn't letting me go alone, and so we went.

As we left the bus, I remembered what a fellow coworker who was an EMT had taught me. He told me never to run at the scene of an accident. He said when your feet run, so does your brain, and you need to stay calm, so I walked. As we passed the front of the bus I realized the futility of the first aid kit and tossed it aside. I slowly approached the man lying on his side in the ditch and kneeled down beside him. He wasn't breathing. As I put my hand on his shoulder to turn him over to start CPR, he let out a big sigh and started to breathe. He also started to shake, so I took off my coat and covered him with it. I'll never forget what happened next. The high school student took off his new black leather coat and covered the rest of the man. He never even thought about it; he just did it. I ran back to the bus to radio in, "He's alive! Tell them to get that damn ambulance here, and send a helicopter!"

Mike pulled up and we transferred the kids to his bus, including my 10-month-old son who was riding in his car seat and my four other children. I waited and shivered and froze in the cold October wind in my thin flannel shirt. But, even so, I shook more from shock than the cold.

A pickup truck pulled up from the same direction the motorcyclist had come. A big, burly man got out, and I recognized him from my days driving stock cars. He said, "I knew it was going to get him some day."

I had the presence of mind to ask, "What was going to get him?"

He answered, "Running the stop signs. I told him it would get him one of these days."

Incredulously, I looked at him and asked, "He did this all the time?"

The man nodded yes and then told me it was his uncle.

I told him his uncle was still alive and he should go down by him. He stammered, "No, no," and said he lived about a mile down the road and that his uncle had just left his house. He got back into his vehicle, turned around, and drove off.

I stood there in disbelief, alone once more, in the cold, icy wind. A fellow bus driver got to the scene shortly after that in a borrowed truck. It seems he heard the call on the radio and somehow had switched from his busload of kids to a borrowed pickup truck. He was a local firefighter and was a welcome sight indeed. He proceeded to start first aid. I saw him place gauze over an oozing wound on the motorcyclist's temple, just under my jacket collar.

The police arrived and I was asked to sit in the cruiser and give a statement. The officer, ironically, was a high school classmate of mine. He asked how I was doing and I said just fine, until now. As he filled out the forms, I saw the helicopter and ground ambulance arrive. More EMTs. One asked if I was okay, and I answered yes, I was.

I suddenly knew that the man was dead. Don't ask how, I just knew. I sensed him above us. I sent a thought message and said I was sorry. "I tried to avoid you, but I couldn't." Nothing short of ditching the bus would have worked, and the ditches were steep on the left side of the road. A thought message came back, "I know, it's okay. I know you tried, I forgive you." That meant a lot to me, and I felt a huge sense of relief.

Another officer came over and whispered, "Get her out of here," but he wasn't as quiet as he thought. The officer asked my boss, who was now on the scene, to take me back to the bus station. We left in his pickup truck and headed back to the office. I was asked to take a drug and alcohol test, and complied. As we left the company to head to a local medical center for the test, I watched the helicopter fly over, heading to the hospital.

I passed the Breathalyzer, but we had to wait a day for results of the drug screening. As a result, I was grounded and unable to drive my route the next morning. Just as well, I thought. I didn't think I should have driven in my current mental state anyway.

My husband picked me at the bus company that evening after the testing and drove home. Now I had to shift gears and make dinner. Great. I had planned on hotdogs. And I had to serve ketchup, too. I choked down a hotdog, but was unable to use my favorite condiment for about three months.

As I waited with my kids in the driveway the next morning for another driver to pick them up, I remember thinking how beautiful the sunrise would have looked on any other day.

Mike arrived, got off the bus, and hugged me in front of a busload of kids. I was embarrassed, but it did me a world of good.

I walked back into the house and remembered I had promised to send cookies to school today for the bake sale. Might as well, I thought. It'll help if I keep busy.

I got started and then it happened — another thought message. "Cookies? You're making damn cookies?" I was shocked. I could feel his presence above me. I continued baking, then packed them up and drove to school. I dropped them off in the office, taking the time to explain to the secretary why I was doing it, that a deal's a deal, and the kids were counting on me. It seemed to appease him, but I could still feel his presence above me.

After I arrived back home, the phone rang. I didn't want to talk to anyone, so I didn't answer it. It rang again a while later and I decided I might as well answer, or they'll just keep calling. It was a floral company that wanted directions to my house for a delivery. I gave it to them, all the while thinking that whoever was sending this should be sending it to the motorcyclist's family, not to me. A little while later, the florist delivery truck arrived with a pretty balloon and soup mug arrangement from my boss. Later, as I picked up the newspaper, I saw that the other phone call had been from the newspaper, where the bus's picture was now plastered over the front page. There was fluid spilled under the bus. I knew it was power steering fluid, but the average reader wouldn't. Later, I found out that a neighbor who lived 50 or so feet from the accident scene had called the reporter to come cover the story. She apparently expected to get a reward for the tip. Somehow, mercifully, the reporter had gotten lost and didn't get there until after I had left. I couldn't imagine what I would have done with his camera if he showed up and shoved it in my face while I waited there, alone. (Oh, yes I could!) The neighbor was quoted in the newspaper as saying, "The driver was going way too fast, and didn't exit the bus right away to help the motorcyclist. The driver only walked nonchalantly, didn't even run." She had effectively crucified me. And where was she when it happened? She didn't offer help or even do something as simple as bring a blanket to cover the man. How about the kids? Did she even care if they were hurt? Apparently not. The newspaper stated that they were unable to reach the driver that morning for comment.

I waited for the kindergarten bus later that morning with my five-year-old. The driver got out and came over — another hug. I have friends, I thought.

I decided to replace the jacket of the student who had helped me and asked him where he bought it. I went to the store and picked one up and drove it to his house. Therapy for me, I guess. He thanked me but said he couldn't accept it, and that, no offense, but this wasn't the same jacket but a cheaper version and that the bus company should replace it, not me. As I returned it, the clerk asked why I was returning it. I spilled my guts and told her the whole story. She had a shocked look on her face as my story unfolded.

She said, "My best friend is the one who passed you. She lives a couple of miles farther down that road. She was mortified to realize that if had she not passed you, it could have been her, with much different results."

My boss asked if I wanted my coat back, and I told him it was a favorite jacket of mine, but still, I was very uncertain about it. He picked it up and gave it to me at work. I dropped the plastic bag it was in on the kids' picnic table in the kitchen when I got home. Later, when I picked up the bag and flipped it over, I saw, "Caution, blood — biohazard." I also saw leaves and the piece of gauze from the motorcyclist's temple still stuck to the collar. I instantly recoiled and dropped the coat to the floor. Then I hauled it out to my bus, shoving it out of sight under the driver's seat. I went back in and used liquid bleach to scour the kids' picnic table.

Later, I dropped the bag and its contents into the Dumpster at work, tossing it to the far back corner. There was some garbage in there already, but not a lot.

The next time I stopped at work to fuel, I looked into the Dumpster as I dumped the trash from my bus. The Dumpster was fuller, the jacket still there. The following time I stopped to fuel, the jacket was gone, with an obvious empty spot where it had been. To this day I don't know who or what removed that jacket, but I know someone, or something, did.

By reading the obituary, I found out that the motorcyclist was actually a man my husband and I had worked with some years back. In fact, he had trained my husband on his very first job and they had worked together for quite some time and were good friends. The motorcyclist had been retired for a while by the day of the accident, however. I decided to go to both the wake and the funeral. My husband volunteered to go with me, and I was glad for the support. Going alone would have been hard, but I was determined to see this thing through. At the wake, when I entered the room, a hush fell, and all eyes stared at me. As I looked into the casket, I was immediately whisked back to the scene of the accident, as if someone had dropped a nuclear bomb directly in front of me.

I saw the burly nephew and knew I needed to talk to him. It was important to me. I tried to walk up to him, but he turned his back to me and continued to ignore me while carrying on a conversation with someone else. I was devastated. Then I looked up and saw the EMT who had inquired if I was okay at the scene of the accident, and she smiled. I tried twice more to talk to the burly nephew, only to have him again, both times, turn his back to me, and finally we left. The funeral the next day went better and I swear the priest knew I was there because it seemed he directed a portion of his speech at me. I left feeling a whole lot better.

As I was breastfeeding my son late one night, a thought message came, "Suckling babe, at the breast." Suckling babe? I thought, nobody talks like that anymore, but I knew where the message had come from. He continued to hang around me sporadically, and I now felt his extreme dislike of me, since I was the one responsible for putting him "there." Apparently, he was not in a forgiving mood anymore. The most bothersome and unnerving time would be when he would hover over me in the shower in the evening. I guess a person always feels most vulnerable when they are naked. I know I would much rather have to defend myself fully clothed. I could always feel his presence above me in the late evening, after the rest of the family was in bed, almost as if he wanted to taunt and torment me. I came to dread darkness and I knew he was starting to get to me. I would see visions of his limp body sailing through the air from the front of the bus over to the ditch. Just as soon as his body would land, the motorcycle would come back into view and the "movie" would run again. I had to mentally sweep it into a closet and lean against it forcefully to stop it.

One evening as I made my nightly hot chocolate, I headed to my favorite chair, but stooped to pick up a small toy from the kitchen floor. A small amount of hot chocolate spilled onto the floor. To my horror, it formed the perfect likeness of his face twisted in fear that day. It was terrible. The thought message came, "Go ahead and drink it now if you can." I sent my thought message back instantly in a burst of anger. "Watch me! I'm tired of this, and I want my hot chocolate." I went to my chair; he followed and stewed above me as I drank it. Still, I thought I could feel his respect after I stood up to him.

My youngest sister stopped by one day, and, as we stood in the doorway, I told her what had been happening. I whispered into her ear that I could feel him above us. She said she had met the strangest woman, someone to whom our mother had just sold a house. (My mother and sister both worked in real estate.) The woman had interested my sister in something called dowsing. My sister said she had taken a course through this woman on a whim, and felt confident she could "dowse" this guy out of my life. Dowsing was supposed to work by holding a pendulum object in your right hand. You would ask it questions, and, by the way it swung, you would get your answer. You were always supposed to ask if what you were doing was in your best interest and ask your Higher Power to help you achieve it. You were never to proceed if it was not in your best interest to do so. We set up a time to try it, because by this time I was desperate for some relief.

My sister started by telling me that we had to ask it two simple questions first, one obvious yes question and one obvious no. That would show us which answer it was giving when the pendulum swung. If it didn't know the answer, it was supposed to swing aimlessly in circles.

I was skeptical, but it seemed to work for her. I even put my hand over her wrist to make sure she wasn't moving the thing with her own muscles, but she wasn't. This thing was, unfortunately, not only able to communicate with good spirits, but also evil ones could sneak in along with the intended contact spirit. As I held the pendulum in my hand, I felt a slight shudder, then absolutely nothing. My sister was afraid to do the dowsing alone, so she kept calling this woman and getting advice on how to proceed and what to ask.

I was told to recite some lines about how I wanted this person to leave me alone and how I wanted to let go of all thoughts of the accident. Then my sister was to ask it to go towards the light and leave. We did all of this, and I felt a tremendous sense of relief. I'm glad we did this in broad daylight.

The woman then said before she hung up that my sister should be careful, that sometimes the evil ones get even with you for meddling by attacking those close to you, such as pets. Wonderful, we thought. My sister left.

That night I took a shower alone for the first time in weeks. It was great. Unfortunately, my oldest daughter hurried out of the shower way sooner than normal and said she felt very uncomfortable in there, almost as if someone were above her, watching. I thought angrily, now he's bothering her. My sister's voodoo, as I had come to call it, had successfully gotten him away from me only to have him follow and harass my daughter.

My sister called to say she had found two cats dead outside her home. No obvious signs of attack or struggle. She was scared, she said, and worried "they" might go after her husband or their dog next. She said she had destroyed the pendulum and had talked to her priest about it. He advised her to never mess with this dowsing again.

I asked God to please make "him" go away and especially make him leave my daughter alone. My daughter said she felt that presence only a couple of times more in the shower, and then it was gone, never to return, much to her relief.

About this time, the balloon started losing its zip and I decided it was time to share it with the motorcyclist, so I sent a thought message upward saying, "I'm sending it up, watch for it. I hope it gives you a little bit of a lift like it did for me." I opened the patio door and watched as it slowly took off, then swirled ever higher. I watched until I could see it no more. Once again, I felt a tremendous sense of relief.

To this day, my sister swears if she picks up any swinging object, she feels she could use it to dowse but rejects the urge. As for the strange woman who bought a house from my mother, my sister says she doesn't have a clue where she is now.

The woman had told my sister that I was probably a "light" person and that was why I was feeling all the sensations of someone around me. A light person can sense spirits around them, much as an animal can. The average person wouldn't notice a spirit hanging around if they walked through the thing.

I received no further thought messages or strange sensations of any kind after that day. Until today, that is, as I am writing this, and things started happening, like when I'd try to use the Delete key on my computer to get the next line to move up and fill in behind three words I had edited out, and it wouldn't budge. And any further words I would type into that line would move down to the line below. I finally gave up, exasperated, and found a way to end the sentence right there and go to a new paragraph. Probably just my imagination, right? Or was it?

It's late. I think I'll go have that hot chocolate now.

 Charley has also written two young-adult novels, *Girls! Girls! Girls!*, which she self-published, and *Dustin's Debut*, which was published by Press-tige Publishing Company. Charley lives in central Wisconsin with her family. She is currently pursuing a degree in Business and writing another young-adult novel. She is also pursuing a career in freelance writing.

The House Ghosts

Rae Nell Causseaux

We crested a hill and saw the two-story cottage surrounded by trees. I couldn't believe this was the house Mrs. Nix, the real estate agent, had told us about. The price on the information sheet was much too low for a place like this. The owners had already moved and Mrs. Nix let us into the almost empty house. I say almost because there was a great deal of junk left scattered about, as if the owners had left in a hurry. It had been originally built as a simple summer lake cottage. There would have to be numerous improvements to make it a year-round home, but we were a do-it-yourself family. The needed repairs and insulating didn't discourage us. The location was perfect, and the price wonderfully affordable.

We moved in on the Fourth of July, and truly had something to celebrate. At last we were in the country with a lake close by for swimming and boating, and four bedrooms so that each of our three children would have their own room.

The first couple of years were a little rough until we finished the remodeling to make the house warm in winter and cool in summer. Nothing unusual happened until we built a den, dining room, and utility room onto the house. The den was 15 by 24 feet. Now we had lots of room for parties, friends, and family. But I guess HE didn't approve of the addition to HIS house.

The den was only partially finished. There was no carpet or paneling yet. I loved the vaulted ceiling and openness of the room. One night after everyone else was in bed asleep, I curled up in a chair in the far corner of the den to read. The book was really good, and I became so engrossed I didn't notice the passage of time. When the chill in the room seeped into my awareness, I looked at my watch. It was almost midnight. I closed the book, got up, and started across the den. Halfway across the room I walked into a cold, transparent wall. I really banged into it. I wear glasses, and they were painfully jammed back on my face. Anyone who wears glasses understands how badly that hurts. Stunned? Dazed? For a brief moment I didn't know what I felt. I put my hand out and pushed on the obstacle before me. It gave a little, like cellophane, and was so cold I had to jerk my hand back. Did the stark terror start at my head or feet? I don't remember. I just remember it traveling from one end of my body to the other. I'd never felt fear like that.

I didn't realize I was holding my breath until my mind yelled at me, "Take a breath." I exhaled and inhaled quickly. When my legs finally responded to the orders they had been ignoring, I backed into the corner and sat back in the chair. I began to hear a chuckle that seemed to come from the empty space before me. From somewhere deep within me, anger began to grow. This was our home, the home we had dreamed of, the home we had worked hard for. My fear was pushed aside by this anger.

"Now just a damned minute. I don't know what you're trying to pull, but it's not going to work. This is our home. You aren't going to run us off. If you want to stay here, you have to behave yourself. Now, you're going to take that wall, or whatever it is, away and never put it back up again. Don't give us any trouble and we won't give you any trouble."

The chill in the room slowly faded. When my legs felt like they would cooperate, I stood up and very slowly walked across the room with my hand outstretched and out of the den. Sleep was elusive the rest of the night. I didn't tell my family about the incident, thinking there was no need to frighten them.

That should have been the last of our cold guest, but of course it wasn't. His next game involved an old mirror.

The mirror held a mystery. After my father-in-law's death, we found it wrapped in an old quilt on the top shelf of his coat closet. The carved wooden frame and overall design of the mirror led us to believe it was an antique. We wondered why such a lovely thing was stored away and not on a wall. We took it home and found the right place for it on the living room wall. It was located perfectly for a quick check of appearance before walking out the front door.

One busy morning I did just that before leaving to run errands. My hair was a little mussed so I dug my comb out of my purse to straighten it. As I pulled the comb through my hair, I saw in the mirror a man walk behind me. He looked straight ahead and seemed in a hurry. I jumped and turned. There was no one in the room.

"Good morning," I addressed the empty room. "I see you decided to stick around. Well, thanks for not causing any trouble."

Over the next few months, everyone in the family saw him in the mirror at one time or another, as he hurried across the living room. We became so accustomed to the image, we would just acknowledge him with a greeting and go on with our business. Other people who saw him didn't always take it so calmly. A scream from a guest in the living room would let us know our resident ghost had just passed through the room.

Two or three years after our original meeting in the den, he was joined by another being. Friend? Playmate? This one preferred to hang out upstairs most of the time. It was full of mischief, and would torment and tease. Things would go missing, such as billfolds, glasses, and books. They would turn up in weird places like on top of the bathroom light fixture or on the top shelf of the kitchen cabinet. It was always someplace high, and a chair or stool was needed to retrieve the missing object when it was found.

This was tolerated with moderate grumbling, but the next stunt was too much for my son Phillip, who was twelve at the time. One day after school, he went to his room upstairs and immediately came charging back down. He ran into the kitchen and grabbed my arm. He was white-faced and trembling.

"I'm not going back up there." His tone of voice was one I had never heard before. He meant it.

"What's wrong?"

"My whole room is changed around and there's a coffin in the middle."

Of course I dropped whatever I was doing, and ran up to his room. Nothing was moved. There was no coffin.

"There's no coffin up here," I called down to him. "Everything's the same as it was this morning when I came up for your laundry. Which, by the way, you were supposed to bring down before you went to school."

I'm serious, Mom. There *was* a coffin. I'm not going back up there. I'll sleep on the couch, or the floor, or anyplace. But not up there."

My daughter Jeanne agreed to change rooms with Phillip. We moved all his things down and hers up. Our playful spirit didn't get very far in frightening Jeanne. It would hop around her room at night in the form of a tiny bright red light. It would knock things over and wake her up. She always kept something on her night table to throw at it. They played that game until she was grown and left home to get married.

After all the children were grown and gone, we were host to a young couple from out of town. (I'll call them Joe and Carol but those aren't their real names.) We were friends of Joe's parents. They were to stay with us until he was settled in his new job and they could find a place of their own.

We told them about the possible things that might happen in that upstairs room so they wouldn't get frightened. Joe laughed and said they didn't believe in nonsense like that.

The first morning when they came downstairs, Joe said there was a problem with the wiring. The light kept coming on all night, and he had to keep getting up and turning it off.

My husband asked him if the switch was in the on position each time he got up. It was, so the problem couldn't be wiring.

They moved out a short time later, but before they moved, they had changed their mind about "nonsense like that."

A year or so later we decided to remodel the two small upstairs rooms into a single large master suite for ourselves. Phillip helped with the job. Part of the flooring had to be replaced. When the old boards were up, I was called to come upstairs.

My husband and Phillip stood by the hole staring at an old black pillbox hat with a net veil. It had rested for years, presumably since the house was built, between the downstairs ceiling and the upstairs floor. Neither would touch it. They said it gave them a creepy feeling each time they reached for it. I was able to pick it up with a piece of broken board and throw it in the trash. After that, our mischievous friend never returned. The man downstairs was still there years later when we moved. I guess I should have told the new owners about him, but since we took the mirror with us, I didn't think they would ever know he was there.

The house we moved to has a delightful ghost, Katie. She's the original owner that the house was built for. She lived into her 90s and, from what I've been told by neighbors, was quite a character. When she was in her 80s, she would dress in costume for Halloween and go trick-or-treating at her friends' homes. The children from streets around knew her as the cookie lady. She was a very good cook and often helps me. I wasn't a good cook before I moved here, but I've improved greatly. Old-fashioned recipes that I never cooked before come into my head and onto the table deliciously. When my husband tastes a new dish, he looks into the kitchen and says, "Thank you, Katie." She's not here all the time, but I can feel when she is. Sometimes I catch a glimpse of her from the corner of my eye when she crosses a room. She's happy we're here with all the hustle and bustle of the children and grandchildren visiting.

You may wonder why ghosts, spirits, or whatever you call paranormal beings, don't frighten or upset me anymore. I think the fear I felt when I ran into that cold wall so many years ago used up my lifetime supply of fear. Or maybe it's because I accept them as being there, so they accept me.

If I ever move again, I hope the house I move to has an interesting ghost. It makes living there more fun.

In the sixth grade Rae Nell Causseaux decided to become a writer after she won a fountain pen in an essay contest. Getting married and having children put a hold on that plan, but gave her many life experiences to express in poetry. She has had numerous poems published. The quiet country life by Lewisville Lake in North Texas is just right for her now. "My computer and I spend many happy hours together," she says. Her first novel, *Search For A Beginning*, was published in 1998. As an active member of the Denton Writers League, Rae Nell has found talented friends in the area who love reading and writing as much as she does. Her family has grown to include grandchildren and great-grandchildren. Each day she looks at her world and says "Aho Maheo," which is Cheyenne for "Thank you, God."

Locked Out

Sean Swank

I t all started because I was bored. Looking for something to read, I grabbed a book of Texas ghost stories from my roommate's bookshelf. As I browsed through its pages, I became engrossed in the fantastic tales of ghostly encounters. In San Antonio, the ghosts of children killed when a train collided with their stalled school bus, push cars over railroad tracks. In nearby Wimberley, the ghosts of divers in Jacobs Well manifest as spheres of light and chase visitors in the nearby cemetery. And in my own hometown of Austin, a woman committed suicide in room 319 of the Driskill Hotel after a shopping spree, and her ghost, laden with shopping bags, has been seen in front of the door to that room.

By the time I finished reading the book, I had a new hobby. I live in an old and haunted town and I was determined to learn as much as I could about Austin's haunted restaurants, graveyards, and hotels. For the next few months, I read more books and visited the locations of documented sightings. I photographed local cemeteries during full moons, walked through ancient buildings, and even checked into the Driskill Hotel for a night. For all of my eagerness and diligence, the only thing that haunted me was my credit card bills.

Last summer, I talked my roommate into going on a ghost tour. The ad promised a history tour of Austin's most haunted sites based on years of research and personal experience. Erik and I arrived at the appointed time and location, a small coffee shop near the state capitol building. We expected to fight a crowd for a position near the front, but when we walked in, only two other living souls occupied the small space — a pregnant woman with long, straight black hair and a young-looking man dressed boots to hat in black Gothic garb.

I asked about the haunted tour and the man in black extended his hand and said, "You must be Sean." He introduced himself as Maverick and told us that the rain usually kept people away from outdoor walking tours, but he was happy to give Erik and me a private tour. We headed out the door and turned onto Austin's infamous party headquarters — Sixth Street.

Maverick was leading me through familiar territory. For the past eight years, I had frequented Sixth Street. I celebrated my 21st birthday there, met more than a few girlfriends, and have patronized almost every bar in the area. But I'd never seen a ghost.

Erik and I were given the royal treatment. Because it was just the three of us, Maverick took his time with the tour, escorting us to places that he doesn't usually include on the tour.

We walked into a bar in the heart of Sixth Street called Casino El Camino — locally famous for one of its bartenders, Mr. Lifto, who had a stint with the Jim Rose Circus lifting heavy objects with his...um...Casper. I had been to the bar a few times, but that night it felt different. Maybe because I was charged up from months of fruitless ghost hunting or maybe because it was the kind of dreary night that makes a person want to take his own life. I don't know what I expected to happen, but it certainly wasn't what did happen.

It was relatively early — Sixth Street doesn't get going until midnight — and we found a table and ordered drinks. Maverick explained that many years ago the downstairs area of the bar had been a family-owned grocery store and bar, and the family's living quarters were upstairs. Three of the family members — the owner and two of his daughters — had died in the building. These were not violent deaths. They had been struck by an unknown illness and never recovered. I had always believed that a ghost haunted a place if he or she had suffered torture and strangulation, or been bludgeoned, or died in some other horrible way. Dying slowly from what I imagined to be a flu-like illness didn't qualify as bad and I was eager to move to the next place, but our drinks had only just arrived.

Our cocktail waitress, Robin, overheard Maverick's story and added accounts of more strange happenings — pool balls appearing on top of the coin-operated tables when the entire bar was empty; ashtrays whizzing across the room late at night; doors locking inexplicably. Robin's stories could have been part of a haunted script that she and Maverick had cooked up ahead of time, but I wanted to believe them. I had been searching for ghosts for months and here they were, right under my nose.

Erik and I left Maverick at the table in search of the mysterious locking door. Robin had directed us toward the back of the club, past zebra-patterned walls to a staircase that led to the pool room upstairs, referred to by the staff as the "Diablo Room." Diablo is Spanish for devil. The room was empty of people and discernable devils, and surprisingly cool for a muggy summer night, and I shivered slightly as we crossed the room and examined the door.

It's a wooden door with glass inset windows and opens onto a staircase that leads down to a small courtyard. The thing about the lock is that it isn't a modern key-based lock. It's a complicated antique device that requires a four-step process to secure. Slamming the door, or random vibrations from crowds of drunken people or errant pool balls hitting the floor couldn't possibly trip the lock. It had to be locked from the inside and it had to be locked on purpose. Robin told us that late at night when she was outside collecting empty beer bottles and overflowing ashtrays, she sometimes heard the lock engage, but when she looked through the window into the room, she saw no one.

This night, the door was unlocked and we went through it and down to the courtyard. As we reached the bottom of the steps, we passed a couple on their way up. When the couple tried to open the door, it was locked! It couldn't have been more than 30 seconds from the time Erik and I closed the door behind us to the time the couple discovered that the door was locked. We were certain that no one was in the room behind us. Erik and I rushed up the stairs and asked the couple if they had seen anyone in the room when they peered through the window. They shook their heads and then headed downstairs. To them the locked door was an inconvenience, but to me it was my first haunted encounter! I was reeling.

Earlier, Robin had told us that the bar staff had named the ghost in the Diablo Room "Mary" because the ghost seemed like a girl and she seemed like a Mary. They had given her that name before they knew the history of the building. One of the little girls who died upstairs was named Mary. I wondered what the little girl was trying to lock out of her house. Perhaps the sickness that caused her family so much suffering or her inevitable death. Or perhaps she was trying to keep someone inside.

A couple of weeks later I showed up for Maverick's first Haunted Pub Crawl. With alcohol a prominent part of the evening, the tour was comprised mostly of college kids eager to flip from bar to bar without paying a cover charge. Ten of us gathered at the coffee shop and after a short introductory speech, Maverick kicked off the tour.

For this outing, I was equipped with a 35 mm camera loaded with high-speed film, an electromagnetic field detector (EMF), a non-contact laser thermometer, and much more knowledge about the proclivities of ghosts and spirits. I learned that these entities give off an electromagnetic discharge and an EMF measures that discharge. I also learned that because spirits are electromagnetic, they require a lot of energy to materialize, producing a discernable "cold spot" in an otherwise warm room. A laser thermometer provides an instant temperature reading.

It was a cloudless September evening and the temperature hovered around 85 degrees. We went to a few of the places Maverick had taken Erik and me on our first tour. In each bar, I used my EMF and thermometer, but detected nothing unusual. We entered Buffalo Billiards, a pool hall a few doors up from Casino El Camino. Buffalo Billiards is housed in a building erected in the 1800s and used to be a casino and bar. No one knows how many people were killed over card games or loose women, or how many spirits haunt the bar, but the stories are rich and varied.

After we ordered drinks, Maverick rounded us up near a bar at the back of the club. He began to describe experiences that some of the club's employees have reported — moving shadows, pool balls on top of the table (apparently a favorite trick of pool hall ghosts), and a constant pounding on the upstairs bar late at night. When a bartender sets a drink on top of the bar, the pounding stops. No sooner did Maverick say, "Ghosts will do anything for attention," than a shelf of martini glasses crashed onto the bar. My EMF detector went crazy, squawking loudly, and the needle on the gauge shot to the right. I had just taken a reading at that bar and the EMF had been stone quiet!

One of the last stops was Casino El Camino. While everyone ordered drinks at the downstairs bar, I took my ghost hunting toys upstairs to the Diablo Room. I hadn't been back since that first night when I encountered the locked door. The room was empty when I walked in, but I felt something in the air. The hair on my arms stood up and my skin prickled. It wasn't sinister, but there was definitely an energy in that room. I first swept the area with my EMF but didn't get any sort of positive reading. I then scanned with the laser thermometer. My first digital temperature reading was 69 degrees.

Tour people started gathering upstairs for Maverick's tale, and I continued to scan the room with my thermometer, getting similar temperature readings — 69, 72, 73. I walked toward the locking door and watched aghast as the temperature dropped to 32 degrees. Freezing! I couldn't believe my eyes. I had locked onto a cold spot. The hair on the back of my neck was beginning to stand up and the conversations quieted. I think the others sensed something too. I was excited and nervous, but I had the sense to check my findings. I pointed the thermometer away from the door and the temperature read 69 degrees. I pointed it toward the door and it dropped to 31 degrees. The thermometer was still aimed at the door when the reading suddenly jumped to 70 degrees. Did we disturb Mary as she was about to lock the door?

I've visited the haunted bars and hotels on Sixth Street many times in recent months, but have had no ghostly encounters since my inauguration into the world of the paranormal. I'm not disappointed, though. I know where to find Mary. And like a Boy Scout, I'm always prepared with my EMF and laser thermometer for my merit badge in the unbelievable and unknown.

Sean Swank is a computer guru in Austin, Texas. On his days off, he's an amateur paranormal researcher and a damn fine cook. He would like to thank everyone involved in helping to create this story, both human and otherworldly.

The Ghost of
Winthrop Hall

Sharon Love Cook

The story has all the elements of a classic mystery: an oceanside mansion, a beautiful young wife, her sailor husband, a shipwreck. What remains is the ghost and its lonely vigil. But first, a little background information:

In 1994 I was editor of the campus newspaper at Endicott College, a school of 1,200 students located in Beverly, 20 miles north of Boston. With Halloween approaching, I needed some "scary" stories and didn't have to look very far, for it seemed everyone had either heard — or witnessed — the Ghost of Winthrop Hall.

Among the many charms of Endicott College's seaside campus are its buildings, many of them historically significant. Winthrop Hall, a sprawling mansion perched high above the Atlantic, serves as a dorm. A Georgian mansion, it was named for John Winthrop, the first governor of Massachusetts, and is one of the oldest houses on Boston's North Shore. A dungeon lies under the library floor, its door concealed. Years ago, slaves escaping to Canada were hidden there.

When I made inquiries about the ghost, I was told to speak to Denise, then director of student development. She had reportedly seen "the lady in blue," as the ghost was called. Nonetheless, when I contacted her, she was reluctant to talk about ghosts, and certainly not for the campus newspaper. In any event, before hanging up, she remarked, "By the way, it's the lady in pink, not blue."

With a deadline approaching, I reluctantly put the tale aside, although I never lost interest in the intriguing ghost tale.

Five years later, while writing for a local newspaper, I decided to resume my investigation into the Winthrop Hall ghost and went straight to one of the earliest recorded sources. Eleanor Tupper, Ph.D, who founded Endicott College in 1939, wrote about the school's history in her book, *Endicott and I* (Cricket Press, 1985).

Dr. Tupper, a no-nonsense professional with a strong Lutheran background, lived at Winthrop Hall with her family during her years as president of the college. On page 63 of her book she deals with the ghost in her characteristic head-on manner. She writes:

> The students believed a legend that a beautiful lady dressed in blue came and went from the cellar area of Winthrop. Each year some girls would see her... One incident occurred that gave our family pause. Our daughter, Priscilla, then seven years old, had never heard talk of ghosts but one twilight she sat alone on the Winthrop porch near the stairs leading to the lawn. As she tells it, a "lady in blue" rounded the corner from the north side of the house and moved along the porch and approached her. The image was clear, not transparent, and Priscilla was looking calmly at first but then realized the lady had no legs and was

unusually quiet. As the lady floated closer, Priscilla beat a hasty retreat. Since then, several students and a housemother have seen the unearthly visitor.

Perhaps the young girl in her fright had mistaken the dress color, because those who are familiar with the ghost invariably say she is dressed in pink. On the other hand, maybe it is not so unusual for ghosts to have a change of wardrobe.

Liz Atilano, then director of the college's career center, enthusiastically discussed the "pink lady," as she called her, with me. From 1981-83 Atilano was resident director of Winthrop Hall and thus knowledgeable about the old mansion's legends. According to Atilano, the ghost suffered from a broken heart. She said:

"Many years ago, the young mistress of the house would pace the wide veranda that faces the open sea, hoping to catch a glimpse of her husband, whose ship sailed past on its way to Salem Harbor. Legend claims that a storm arose and she witnessed his boat become shipwrecked upon the jagged rocks not too far away from her porch. Heartbroken, she hung herself from the beams, leaving behind a ghost who walks the corridors of the house."

Atilano claims that one of the ghost's trademark rituals involves a painting hanging in the foyer, a large landscape of a tree reflected in a pond. When the ghost is present, the painting is found upside down. "I have seen the painting turned many, many times. Each time I heard her footsteps. Even when I was the only one in the building, I heard keys rattling. Students also reported seeing her," she said.

Atilano never considered the Winthrop Hall ghost to be a threatening presence. "It wasn't like the movies. There were no moans and groans. She was never scary. I think she was there to welcome us."

Pink ladies or pink elephants? A cynic would assume the latter, although the people I interviewed were all levelheaded individuals. In fact, Al Cipriani, a former Beverly police officer and, at the time of our interview, a long-term employee in the maintenance department, had heard the rumors. While he never directly saw the ghost, he was aware of its presence while working at Winthrop Hall during the summer months when the college was closed. "We were alone, working downstairs in the rec room and we'd hear footsteps above us and on the stairs. The house was locked. There was no one but us in the building."

It is no surprise that ghost stories should arise from the area in question. The land, after all, dates back to Puritan times and played an important part in the witch trials of neighboring Salem. The Endicott College Library archives contain background information on the land surrounding the college.

It was a crisp autumn day when I sat down with a bulging folder containing old, faded records collected by local and college historians. What I learned helped explain the ghost story in terms of the area from which it evolved, particularly the woods behind Endicott College. On maps, both old and current, this area is called Witch's Woods, named for those accused of witchcraft years ago in nearby Salem. Many tortured individuals sought shelter within the dark, dense woods. One historian writes: "The woods were thought to be haunted."

Around that time, the daughter of wealthy landowner John King, who lived at Thissellwold, the estate that is now Winthrop Hall, told a fantastic story. In the company of her maid and her cousin, she went up to Witch's Woods for a picnic. Though they'd visited the spot for years, when it was time to go home, they got lost.

According to the young girl's account, they suddenly came upon a ridge and looked down and beheld an old Colonial farmhouse, which they approached to get directions home. However, whenever they neared the house, it would disappear. They finally returned home, confused and frightened (archives: Endicott College, 1962).

Because the Kings were respected in the community, the story was widely reported.

While such stories are captivating, I wanted an eyewitness account from a living, breathing person and after making inquiries, I was told to get in touch with Beverly resident Sally King, who was Endicott's dean of students from 1971 to 1979.

Upon hearing of my mission, King was delighted to talk about the ghost. In fact, she was emphatic in her account. Apparently, while serving as dean of the college, she was invited to a Halloween party hosted by a group of students living at Winthrop Hall.

It was late afternoon when King, accompanied by Barbara Decker, the college's registrar, arrived at Winthrop Hall and was directed downstairs to the recreation room. While they were enjoying the refreshments and Halloween decorations, their attention was diverted. King remembers the incident distinctly. She said: "I swear to God it was a ghost, an apparition, coming down the stairs. All of a sudden there it was, wearing a pink dress."

Both women witnessed the vision. "It wasn't tangible, it was as if it was made of smoke, although every detail was perfectly clear." King adds: "It was the most fascinating thing I've ever seen."

It was a dark and cloudy December afternoon when I visited Winthrop Hall. The students were away on winter break, leaving me free to roam the building. Before dropping me off with the house key, a security guard reminded me that I'd be alone in the house.

"That's what I want," I said with a jaunty wave. I stood outside for a long time looking up at the stucco exterior and red tiled roof. Finally, it was time to explore. In the foyer, I spotted the legendary painting of the tree and its reflection and then slowly climbed the stairs to the third floor. I found the light switch and walked down a long corridor, past students' doors hung with holiday decorations.

A tall window at the end of the corridor offered a thin winter light. I stood before it, gazing down at the long veranda where Eleanor Tupper's daughter had spotted the ghost. The jagged rocks that dotted the cove jutted out from a flat gray sea. The view was the same, unchanged, that the house's occupants had observed over the long years.

While thinking of past occupants, I became aware of a distant tinkling, the sound of chimes, bells, or keys. The vast house suddenly felt smaller and I had the impression that I was not alone. I glanced around for a light switch but it was at the other end of the corridor that suddenly seemed very long indeed. Chiding myself for having an overactive imagination, I started walking down the corridor, my steps getting faster as I passed the row of doors. Upon reaching the stairs, I took them two at a time until I reached the bottom and the foyer. Before slamming the front door behind me, I glimpsed the painting — hanging upside down.

As I scurried up the road, I turned for a final, hasty look. A curtain in a window upstairs moved. I wondered: Was it a draft?

I didn't wait to find out.

 Sharon Love Cook has an MFA in Writing from Bennington College and a BS in Communications from Salem State College. She is currently completing work on her mystery novel *Death Ends a Midlife Crisis.* Over the years she has written columns (mostly humorous) for local newspapers, as well as created cartoons and illustrations. Her work has appeared in publications such as *Alfred Hitchcock's Mystery Magazine, Yankee* magazine, and *Orchard Review.* She has a studio at the historical (though not haunted) Blackburn Building in Gloucester, and lives in Beverly, Massachusetts, with her husband, Oliver, dog Chester, and cat Edith.

Pining

Kelly Steed

It was the summer of 1986. I had decided to take some summer courses instead of returning home from college. A couple of friends found us a place to rent not far from the NMU campus. The house had been built in the late 1800s or early 1900s. It was hard to tell exactly because it had been converted into two flats, an upper and a lower, with the basement serving as a laundry room. That was nothing unusual for Marquette, Michigan, a college town with many professors looking to make a little money on the side. The upper, the larger of the two, was meant for only three renters. To cut down on expenses, four other students and I shared it, doubling up in the two bedrooms, with the odd-girl-out sleeping on the sofa bed.

My room was the size of a walk-in closet, just big enough for a bunk bed, a milk crate dresser, and a clothing rack. It was located on the immediate right of the entryway with an open doorway to the kitchen on the room's left. The living room was straight ahead. A large opening off to the left, which at one time might have contained pocket doors, allowed access to another room of the same size. Straight back along the left wall was another doorway into the kitchen and past it on the rear wall was a doorway leading into the back hallway. On the right was another bedroom much larger than the other with the hall dead-ending in a bathroom, which contained a shower stall rather than the standard tub and shower because of space constraints.

Due to the cramped conditions, Karen decided to open the attic, which had a hatchway in the bathroom ceiling, and see if there was room to store some boxes. She borrowed a ladder from a friend, lifting out the wooden cover, and climbed up with three of the girls waiting below. Steve, Karen's live-in fiancé, wasn't home. She discovered that there were already some boxes up there stacked neatly near the front gable. We were the only tenants in the house, as the other apartment was empty for the break.

I was a history major with visions of generations of occupants leaving things behind in that old house's attic to explore. At my behest, Karen checked out the foreign goods and found a diary. I had her pass it to me through the opening. To my disappointment, it was from the 1970s and was really more of a day planner than a diary. Still, I opened the book, hoping to discover something of historical significance. There were few entries, only a sentence or two in length, spaced sporadically throughout the book. One read, "The cat died today." The entry seemed rather cold for a lost family pet, not even a mention of a name.

Karen handed down some of the boxes for examination. The four of us dug through them like pirates searching for a buried treasure. One of the boxes contained a few photos. One picture was of Lindsey holding the cat, solving the mystery of whose treasures we'd found. The boxes belonged to our landlords. That photo confirmed for me why the diary entry felt so cold; it was Lindsey's cat and Arnold wasn't terribly fond of it. The professors had resided in the house prior to dividing it into apartments. Karen thought that they might have forgotten the boxes were up there and called to remind them. She left the ceiling hatchway open while we readied our things for storage.

That night, we were awakened by bloodcurdling screams that rattled our very souls. It was Brenda on the sofa bed. "Something walked across the bed! I felt it!" She was butt up against the sofa back, legs pulled up, clutching her pillow like a combination chest protector, security blanket, and drool bib. Her eyes danced wildly over her coverlet.

None of us had any pets, so Steve figured that it might have been a mouse. As there was no screen in the kitchen window over the fire escape, it was possible that any small animal could have wandered in. At Karen's prompting, he initiated a search but it was to no avail. Steve volunteered to get a mousetrap and everyone returned to bed.

The next day Karen saw a cat run through the back hall and turn into the kitchen, but when she pointed it out, Steve didn't see a thing. A few days later, I was doing dishes and caught a flash of movement out of the corner of my eye. As I turned, I saw a cat, really nothing more than a transparent white shadow in feline form, jump onto the window sill. It soundlessly climbed out onto the wooden fire escape and vanished in mid-stride. Apparently there had never been a screen on that window. Seeing ghosts is a rather strange experience. In the case of the cat, its visage was accompanied by a solemn stillness that made me feel as if I were the intruder into this time frame rather than the other way around. I wasn't particularly alarmed by it. I'd encountered human ghosts before, a hazard that comes from hanging out at historical sites. It didn't bother me to share a flat with one.

That evening, I told the others what I'd seen. While I believed in ghosts, as did the others, Steve was rather cynical about the whole thing, chalking it up to our imaginations. He was a hardheaded Missouri "show-me" type. He figured with all these stories flying about we were just feeding each other's paranoia. I knew that wasn't possible. We'd just read the journal entry and there hadn't been any discussion of ghosts. The natural assumption was that Brenda's visitor had been a mouse. So until Karen saw the cat, there was no reason to start imagining anything else. Karen was too levelheaded to have such fanciful wanderings of the mind; if she said she saw a cat, then she saw one, and I know what I saw wasn't my imagination.

It was Karen's first encounter with the spirit world, so the whole thing particularly alarmed her. When the owners didn't come pick up the boxes within a few days, she put them on the curb for the trash collector, the practical decision expected of a business major, and sealed the attic without storing a thing. She even sent the ladder back, so no one else could get up there. I had been at work and was furious when I discovered what Karen had done in my absence. "You had no right to do that!"

"If they'd wanted that stuff, they'd have picked it up by now. Besides, they had us clean out the basement, said we could keep anything we wanted, and pitch the rest."

"Yeah, but that stuff belonged to former tenants who never responded to the notices they sent out."

"Well, it's gone now."

I had hoped to find some way to release its soul into the light but in the days that followed, it became clear that the cat's spirit was no longer in the house. It was attached to the personal items, which was why it only appeared after the attic had been disturbed, not an unusual occurrence when a structure has undergone major remodeling. So if you're ever wandering around the Marquette city dump and see a transparent cat, tell it to go to the light.

Kelly Steed is the co-author of the hard sci-fi horror novel *Stasis* (Publish-America, Inc. 2001) about religious beliefs versus the scientific realities of cryonics technology and its inherent dangers. She recently completed her second novel, *Camelot's Revenge*, and has had two nonfiction stories about her paranormal experiences published in *FATE* magazine; a third will be out later in 2003. Her essay "As the Millennium Turned" has been accepted for publication in the anthology *Spiritual Visitations* and "Pick Your Cemetery Companions Carefully" will appear in *Romancing the Spirit's Soul*. Kelly received an honorable mention in The Book Review Café's Best Author Awards 2002. She can be contacted at The Steed Zone: http://home.att.net/~s.c.ninlil.c.b/

The Ghostly Roommate

Whitney Leigh Harris

Three years ago, my son, Harrison, and I moved into a 1950s two-bedroom apartment in Portland, Oregon. The morning after we moved in, Harrison, who was only two at the time, awakened me just before sunup. Something had awakened him. We put on our robes and walked down the fairly long hallway into the living area and sat together on the couch. I gazed silently out the living room window, while my son sat on my lap facing the opposite direction, towards the hallway, with his chin resting on my shoulder. He was still quite drowsy and I struggled to understand his sleepy, mumbled words when I asked him if he wanted breakfast. I decided to sit on the couch a bit longer to let Harrison rest on my shoulder and see if he might go back to sleep. The apartment was totally silent and the only light was the faint glow of the sunrise.

All of a sudden, I felt my son's sleepy head jerk straight up at attention. He was silent for a moment and then I heard the question that sent my heart into my throat. In a startlingly loud, awake voice my son asked, "Mommy, who is that man in the hallway?"

My stomach dropped and I was suddenly gripped by fear. I spun around to face the hallway, fully expecting to see an intruder in our apartment. My son's reaction was so abrupt and so direct that I knew without a doubt *he saw a man*!

It took a couple of seconds for my eyes to adjust to the dark hallway, but I saw nothing. Oh my God, I thought, he must have gone into one of the bedrooms or the bathroom! I considered running out of the apartment, but for some reason I didn't. I told my son to stay on the couch and I walked down the hall. As quickly as I could, I began hitting light switches in the hallways, both bedrooms, and the bathroom. I jerked open closet doors and peeked under the beds. I even checked behind the shower curtain, but there was no one.

Puzzled, but relieved, I returned to my son and asked him to explain what he saw.

"I saw a man, Mommy. Who was that man?"

I started to explain to him that he was mistaken and he saw nothing, but I stopped myself. I knew that he must have seen an apparition of some kind. I told him the man was just visiting, but to tell me if he ever saw him again.

The next morning, when I entered our bathroom, I noticed a dim, red glow near the floor. At first I was startled, but then I quickly realized the electric heater was on. This struck me as strange since I had never used it before. I knew my son didn't turn it on because I never allowed him to go into the bathroom alone. Besides, even if he had attempted to turn it on, the on/off switch, I quickly discovered, was very tricky to grasp, and I knew a two-year-old would not have the dexterity to handle it.

Despite the mystery, I forgot about the heater and went about our morning. As usual, it was still quite dark when my son and I entered the living area to sit on the couch to stretch and cuddle before making breakfast. Only a few minutes into our routine and my son abruptly pointed to the far corner of the living room.

"There's that man again, Mommy!"

This time I tried to remain nonchalant and calmly asked my son about the man.

"What is he doing?" I asked.

"He's just looking at me," said Harrison, seeming a little uncomfortable. Harrison stared intently towards the wall for several seconds as if he was carefully listening to someone speaking to him. He nodded a couple of times and then turned and looked at me as if to say, Did you hear that? Harrison seemed somewhat fascinated by the ghost, but at the same time was uncomfortable.

"Would you like me to ask him to leave?"

"Yes, Mommy," Harrison answered quietly, almost as if he was trying to prevent the man from hearing his answer.

"Man," I said nicely, but firmly, "please leave our home."

I waited a moment.

"Is he gone?" I asked.

"Yes," Harrison said, looking happy and relieved. "Can I watch cartoons now?"

Over the next several weeks, every morning was the same. I would awaken to find the bathroom heater on at full force and Harrison would experience a sighting of our new "roommate." I decided to ask our manager about the person who lived in the apartment before us. She told me an elderly man had moved from the apartment into a nursing home shortly before we moved in. Apparently, he lived alone in the apartment for nearly twenty years.

Perhaps the man died in the nursing home and was drawn back to his former home. Perhaps he was still doing his morning routine. It would make sense, after all, for an elderly person to immediately turn the bathroom heater on, especially given the chilly Oregon mornings.

It made sense to me, but I was still shaken about having a ghost around. Although I could not see the ghost myself, I knew that children were often very psychic and open to all kinds of energy and visions that most adults can no longer access. All that mattered was that the sightings made my child uncomfortable and the extra use of the heater in the bathroom was running up my electric bill!

One morning, after Harrison announced another sighting of the ghost, I decided to once again request that he vacate our apartment.

"Man," I said, with my son watching intently, "we want you to leave our home and not come back. I'm sure you are very nice and it is nothing personal, but we want to live here alone now. Thank you."

During the mornings following my plea to the ghost, the sightings stopped and the heater remained off. It seemed to have worked and we got on with our lives.

A couple of months after the last sighting, my sister and her little Yorkshire terrier, Ziggy, came up from Texas for a weekend visit. I told her about our experiences with the ghost and we had a good laugh about it. I assured her that I was certain he was gone and how happy we were to finally settle into our new apartment. Little did I know that my relief would be short-lived.

My sister and Ziggy slept in the living room their first night. Ziggy was a very quiet, lazy little dog who very rarely barked and tended to be a good sleeper. However, about 5 A.M., my sister was awakened by Ziggy growling and staring down the dark hallway. Assuming Ziggy was simply growling at me or Harrison, she ignored the dog and went back to sleep.

When Harrison and I got up around 7 A.M., Ziggy seemed very nervous and refused to walk anywhere near the hallway. When I asked about his strange behavior, my sister told me that Ziggy had growled at us earlier that morning around 5 A.M.

"But we weren't up at 5," I said. "Harrison slept with me and we did not get up until 7."

"But I went to the bathroom about 6 and the heater was on," said my sister, puzzled.

"He's back!" I exclaimed.

Had the ghost been there all those weeks without making any appearances? Did he return for a visit? This time, I called a spiritual healer I knew who offered me some suggestions. She told me to burn sage throughout the apartment and she taught me a cleansing meditation to do as well. Although I was doubtful, I tried what she suggested.

The mornings following the "cleansing," there were no sightings and no running heater. Weeks turned into months and nothing. Now, three years later, there haven't been any incidences. I believe the man must have finally moved onward, into the light I would assume.

Although I did not actually see a ghost during this experience, it was disturbing to say the least. I'm certain the ghost meant no harm. I'm sure he was wondering what we were doing in his home! The most valuable lesson I learned out of the entire experience was to trust my child's ability to see. Imagine if I had completely disregarded his experience. Imagine how frustrating and terrifying that would have been for him, to know he was alone with his awareness of this eerie visitor. Without a doubt, the next time I move into a home with a past, I'm going to do a bit of spiritual housecleaning before I move one box inside!

Whitney Leigh Harris has been involved in spiritual growth and metaphysical studies and practices for over a decade. She works as a freelance writer and offers intuitive guidance readings to others, with her main focus on empowering single mothers. Whitney and her son, Harrison, live in Portland, Oregon. Whitney can be contacted at bluesunscribe@hotmail.com.

A Message From Beyond

Renie Burghardt

I never knew my real mother. She died of pneumonia at the tender age of nineteen, when I was only a couple weeks old. So my maternal grandmother was my dear "Anya," the only mother I ever knew.

My mother had been my grandmother's only child, and she never quite got over losing her. When I was small, I was told that my mother was in heaven, and that she would always be watching over me. Otherwise, my grandmother never talked to me about my mother. It was just too painful for her, I later realized. But she and my grandfather were loving, valiant, supportive parents, who did everything they could to protect me from the war, and always tried their best to see that I didn't go without.

I didn't know much about my real father either. When I was small, my father was the stranger who occasionally came to visit me at my grandparents' home. I knew he was my father, but he seemed so awkward and shy in my presence that he made me feel uncomfortable.

It was during the spring of 1944 when I last saw my father. He brought me a shiny, new red bike, and he took me for a ride on it. I was seven years old and loved the bike, but when my father asked me for a hug after our ride, I offered a handshake instead.

145

"I know I'm almost a stranger to you, but you are my only child and I love you," my father told me that day. "I loved your mama, too, more than I can ever say. When this war ends, you and I will get to know each other better. I promise you that!" But he never got the chance to make good on his promise, because fate intervened.

All this took place in the Bacska region of Hungary where I lived in 1944, while my young father was in the army. The war he spoke of was World War II, of course, and Tito and his communist partisans were soon breathing down our necks. My grandfather decided to move us to safer surroundings soon afterward. There was no time to notify their son-in-law of our move. Besides, we weren't sure where we would end up.

Of course, so much happened in the next three years, among them the Soviet occupation of Hungary. When we finally managed to escape, we landed in a refugee camp in neighboring Austria. We didn't know where my father was, or if he even survived the war. Finally, in 1951, our hopes for a better life became a reality when we were allowed to immigrate to the United States of America. After we boarded the old Navy ship, the U.S.S. *General Stewart*, in September of 1951, we watched from the deck as the ship pulled out of the harbor in Bremen Haven, Germany.

"We will never see our old homeland again," my grandfather lamented sadly.

"But we're on our way to America, the land of new opportunity!" my grandma added. And it was at that exact moment that I thought of my father and the promise he had made the last time I saw him. I thought how he'd never get the chance to make good on that promise if he survived the war, and I felt sad.

Of course, in America life was soon busy and good. My grandparents went to work and I went to school. I don't know why, but we never talked about my father, and I can't recall even thinking about him. It was like he had never even existed. Then in June of 1954, after I had not seen my father for ten years, someone intervened on his behalf.

One night, in the spring of that year, I had gone to bed as usual, my mind filled with plans for the coming weekend. I was going to a dance, a special boy would also be at that dance, and sweet promise was in the air. Suddenly, out of nowhere, a vision appeared at the foot of my bed. It was a beautiful young woman with long, flowing blond hair, wearing a sad expression on her strangely familiar, lovely face. I sat up and gazed at her, not at all frightened, for though I had never known her, and didn't even have a picture of her, I knew who she was. She was my mother.

"You must get in touch with your father. He is very worried about you, because he doesn't know what has happened to you. He needs to know that you are alive and well so he can go on with his life in peace. You must do this very soon," she said in a voice that was just above a whisper. Then she was gone, vanished into the thin air she had come from.

I sat there on the bed and began to cry. I cried for never having known her, and I cried for my father and all the sadness and worry I had caused him. My grandmother must have heard me, because she came into my room to ask what was wrong. I told her about the vision.

Grandma began to cry, too, as I described the woman that had come to me with a message. And the following morning, my grandfather wrote a letter to some relatives who still lived in the old country, inquiring about my father. Three weeks later I received a jubilant letter from him.

"Though we're separated by a great ocean now, I'm happy and relieved to know that you are alive and well, my dear child. Never forget that I will always love you. And I will always love your mama, too," my father wrote in that first letter. And when I answered his letter, I told him my mama still loved him too, even beyond the grave, for it was true.

Renie Burghardt was born in Hungary and came to the United States as a teenager in 1951. She began freelance writing in 1990, and has been published in many magazines and anthologies, including *Chicken Soup for the Christian Family Soul, Chocolate for Women* (several), *Cup of Comfort, Cup of Comfort for Friends, Cup of Comfort for Women, The Big Book of Angels* (Rodale Press), the *Listening to the Animals* series published by Guideposts, *God Allows U-Turns, Whispers from Heaven*, and many others. She lives in the country and enjoys observing nature, animals, reading, writing, and spending time with her family and friends.

Do You Believe In Ghosts?

Peggye Swenson

When my son stepped off a plane from California, the first words out of his mouth were, "Do you believe in ghosts?"

The question took me aback. Of course I do, but I'd never shared it with my kids who were unaware of the knack. I'd been considered "spooky" since I was a kid and I didn't think that adding that to the list of attributes for my children was a good idea.

"Why do you ask?" I intoned as I tried to think of a way to dance around the question. Then I decided differently. After all, Duane was 32 years old and definitely not impressionable. Before we got in the car, I confessed. "Yes. I believe in ghosts."

"You've seen them?"

Again, I answered in the affirmative. In for a penny, in for a pound. Some things are too important to lie about and I felt my "gift" was one of them. I don't know why I have it or if it means anything, but since I was a kid I've seen people who aren't there, heard sounds that no one else heard, seen places that didn't exist. My mother insisted it was because I was such a heathen. Maybe. But who knows?

Yes, I believe in ghosts, have had many ghostly encounters, and never doubt anyone else's account of the supernatural. Some say I'm too trusting; I consider it a gift that many people have but never talk about. That conversation took over our lives for several days with Duane asking pointed questions. When? Where? What do "they" look like? Why you? I answered as best as I could. Finally, he dropped the subject and we went on with other discussions.

We were slated to go to my mother's for her birthday the next morning when Duane raided the change drawer for a trip to the store for munchies. When he didn't come back by bedtime, I left the outdoor lights on for him and went to bed. After all, he was a grown man. No telling who he'd met or where he'd gone. I knew he'd be back for our trip.

But he wasn't. When I got up early I found the backyard light still on, his bed unslept in, and my car absent. I wasn't thrilled with that aspect. Since we'd been reduced to one vehicle between us, the share-a-ride program had many fits and starts. He'd be home soon, I reasoned.

I was on my second cup of coffee when my dog alerted me we had visitors. I opened the front door to a DPS officer waiting on the porch. He asked my name, and I gave it to him. He asked if I knew Duane Swenson and I replied he was my son. My brain kicked into gear, and instantly I thought he'd been in an accident and my car was crumpled in some ditch while he was in an emergency room without a way home.

"Your son was killed this morning in an accident."

The words that spilled from his mouth didn't make any sense. Duane had gone out for munchies. He'd be back any second. This officer didn't know what he was saying.

But the other half of me realized he was telling the truth. Duane was much too considerate not to be here when we were planning to visit his grandma. Something important had to have held him up. The cop was trying to explain just what that was.

I stopped him. If I was going to hear this, I had to have backup. I called my son Tony and handed the phone to the officer while I sought a chair to hold my quaking body.

My big dog was instantly at my side, glaring at the trooper and threatening mayhem with his growl. I ordered him to sit and be quiet while the officer came back into the room. I could still see him talking to me, but I couldn't hear a word for the roaring in my ears. If I didn't hear it, it wouldn't be true. Lousy logic.

Tony roared into the front yard and scrambled from his car into the house. Tears were streaking down his face as the two of us listened to the officer's words. There was no question of identity. He'd been struck while walking along the highway. He was determined dead at the scene by attending paramedics.

By turn, things moved too fast and far too slow. A gathering of the clan started instantly while I was still trying to find the ground. I walked in a daze, unable to believe what I knew to be true and afraid to be still. If I kept moving, it would all be okay.

The end of the second day. My kids had scattered to stay with other siblings in the area with only my oldest son, Nic, remaining overnight with me. There were still calls to be made but I couldn't think of that. My mind was in neutral as I sat and looked at the wall.

When a California friend called, I slipped into the hall to the spot where I'd put the phone. At my right hand was my bedroom, dark and foreboding. Straight ahead at the end of the hall was Duane's bedroom where a low light burned. It felt safe in the hall as I talked to Mickie. We'd been talking for almost an hour when I noticed something in Duane's room. Someone was sitting on the bed. Not trusting my eyes, I excused myself from the phone call and went for Nic. "Just sit here and tell me what you see," I said, picking up the phone again to relate what was happening before my eyes.

The covers on Duane's bed ruffled as if someone had laid down and the bed bounced as if the person had turned over. I wasn't sure of what I saw, but Nic's strangled "I see it, Mom" strengthened my vision.

We sat in the dark hall for several minutes while the "person" settled himself in bed, bunched the pillow, and settled to sleep.

The scene was too intense for Nic who deserted me for more reasonable space.

In the next several days came more hints that my youngest was still around. I'd lose something — keys, glasses — and when I gave up looking, I'd find them on the table next to my favorite chair. My dog, Sham, would spring to his feet, tail wagging at an empty doorway. I'd hear Duane's distinctive footsteps in the kitchen. All a sign to me that I wasn't alone. The ache of his death still pounded me, but the comfort of his concern eased things.

I didn't return to work for two weeks. I had things to do. Before his death we'd been talking about donating my computer to the Victim's Assistance office. Since his was much more sophisticated than mine, I chose to have a tech come in and clean it before I made the donation.

I was hanging curtains in the back room while the tech was at work. Duane had always been protective about his computer and allowed no one to mess with it. While the tech was cleaning, I heard her talking to herself. "Where did I put that? How did it get there?" This happened several times. When I peeked through the door, I watched as she moved all her tools onto the table next to the computer to finish her work. Since I couldn't help, I went back to my own business. In less than a minute I heard her gasp. I glanced back in the doorway to see her white and shaking, staring at all her tools neatly repacked in the case. Seems Duane was still at work. She finished the job, jammed her implements into her bag, and fled. I could almost hear him giggle with delight.

And tools weren't the only things involved. When I had company at night, Duane made himself known in a dozen ways. If I had the TV on something other than *Star Trek* at 6 P.M., he'd start knocking on the cabinet of the TV to alert me.

Once when Suzanne was spending the evening, she chose his favorite chair. In a few minutes the chair rocked forward abruptly, almost dumping her onto the floor. Later, it began to move side to side. Suzanne hung on for dear life and called out, "I know you don't like me sitting in your chair, but I'm going to do it anyway." After a few more vigorous rocks, the chair stilled again.

Duane's visits continued for another six months. Some days there were more, others none. I spoke into the air, assuring him that it was time for him to move on, I would be all right. I didn't believe it, but I think he did.

There was one last visitation. It was dark and cold and I'd been out on a late assignment. When I made coffee and went to crawl into something warm and wooly, I turned my back on the kitchen, but not before I saw a figure behind me. Sham was at my side, tail wagging, and I knew it was Duane. I glanced at the apparition, which had gained form and substance. Duane smiled and gave me a small salute and vanished.

I'm glad we'd had the chance to share my own feelings of ghosts before he died. He felt comfortable staying around awhile to protect Mom.

Peggye Swenson is a retired award-winning reporter/photographer. As a staff writer for *Front Page* and *Inside* detective magazines in the '50s, she cut her teeth on police investigations with the Los Angeles Police Department. She's a member of Freelance Writers' Network of Fort Worth (Texas) and a 20-year member of Texas Press Women.

You Don't Have to Be a House to Be Haunted

Maria B. Murad

All my life I've had this ability, this capacity, or maybe — for lack of a better word — this "gift" of premonition, what the Irish call second sight. I probably inherited it from my mother. It's something she had, and all my girls, to some extent, also possess it. I see signs of it emerging in my granddaughters; it seems to be passed down from female to female in my family. It's a kind of intuition, sometimes even a foretelling, of what is to be. It's related, I believe, to déjà vu, that feeling that we've lived through a situation before. One theory I've heard suggests that déjà vu is a jog in time: We are reliving a memory of something that perhaps occurred immediately before the situation, but so closely timed we don't realize we've remembered something. It's precognition of a sort, I think. That's one manifestation I have fairly often; I also know nine times out of ten who is on the other end of the phone when it rings. With people I'm close to, I can predict before they say something what they will say. It's not a big thing with me, but one of my daughters has the sight so strong that I'd say she could be a medium if she wanted to.

That's another story, but it scares her and she consciously closes it off.

At other times, I feel things, otherworldly things, and sometimes I see things out of the corner of my eye. Maybe spirits, or souls; I'm not sure. I just know they are not flesh and blood, but they are real. I can't control or summon these capabilities; they come and go depending on my emotional state. Sometimes, I think it's as if a door to another space has opened. I won't say another dimension or anything as alien as that, it's just that I know certain things.

An example: I was in a shoe store in Kolanaki Square in Athens once. The owner of the store waited on me and as I was paying for my purchases she said to me, "You have eyes like a medium. Do you know what I mean?" And when I nodded, she added, "You see things." It was a statement, not a question. In Greece, such things are taken for granted. After all, it's such a short ride north from Athens to Delphi where the oracle spoke to ancient leaders, where priestesses worshipped Athena and Zeus and Poseidon. All over Greece you see the symbol of a blue eye, which is worn on neck chains or on pins to ward off evil spirits.

Few places are as hot and humid in August as Washington, D.C. I was there once with my oldest daughter, Lisa. The temperatures hovered around 99 degrees, but it didn't stop us. I had attended a conference in Virginia, and she went along. We planned to stay free in the apartment of a friend of Lisa's. Pam worked for a congressman and lived very cheaply in the lower apartment of the congressman's row house. Since the congressman went home to Iowa for the summer recess, and Pam did, too, her apartment was empty for a couple months in the summer. Naturally, we jumped at the chance; we could see the city, take some tours, and buy souvenirs, with only meals to pay for.

The apartment was on the street level, laid out railroad style, the rooms running from front to back. The only windows in the place were in the front, and one of them was blocked by a small air conditioner, which only cooled the room marginally. Just beyond the last room, where the washer and dryer stood, was a stairway that led through a locked door to the congressman's dwelling, which stretched up three flights. These old brick townhouses, which often date from the mid-1700s, are tall and narrow, and are built with common walls, similar to some of today's townhouses.

The front door opened directly into the living room. Quite ordinary, nothing to give you pause here, the furniture second-hand, nondescript but comfortable. Passing through a wide arched doorway, you entered what passed for the bedroom. That is, there was no door or separate wall; it might have been a dining room at one time. Pam had placed her large double bed on the left wall, with a night table next to it, and opposite, a dresser with an old mirror. Beyond this room was a small galley kitchen, and then a bathroom, and finally, the aforementioned laundry area.

The apartment got progressively darker as you traversed from front to back rooms. It also grew colder as you moved to the back, too, which seemed unusual in view of the sluggish air conditioner, which barely cooled the air of the living room. It was a peculiar, clammy cold that seeped into your bones.

The bedroom made me edgy and anxious. When I lay down for a nap, or when we retired at night, my sleep was full of dreams. Strange, claustrophobic scenes with people who crowded and frightened me. I would wake several times, glad for consciousness and an awareness that daylight was not far off. The hallway to the kitchen was dark even with lights on, but it wasn't the quality of the light that bothered me. It was the depressive, oppressive feeling that came over me there and in the bathroom. I got in and out of that room particularly fast, because I saw things out of the corner of my eye. They seemed to be figures or shadows, but as soon as I'd turn to see them more clearly, they disappeared. Sometimes I almost caught a glimpse in the mirror, but as quickly, the image would vanish. It's hard to explain the terror I felt in this place. The danger was palpable. There was something here that I could not explain away or ignore.

Lisa felt it too. At first, not wanting to alarm her, I said nothing. She kept pressing me, though. She read my face and my silences easily. Besides, her own alarms had been aroused. "You feel something, don't you, Ma?" she'd ask, and I'd reply, "No, no, nothing. It's just a little dark in here." But I couldn't fool her. Stubbornly, though, because there was so much we wanted to see in this marvelous city and not enough money to do it, we didn't go to a hotel. We lasted through our several days, leaving the house early and coming back as late as we safely could, but neither of us could shake the menace and fear of that house. We talked about it later, and conjectured that maybe someone died here violently and his or her spirit still hangs about. Pam told Lisa it was an old coach house back in Revolutionary times, with many travelers stopping by. Pam herself experienced some strange phenomena, too, but she evidently didn't feel threatened or she would have moved.

There were warning signs, of course. There always are, but sometimes if I'm not concentrating or not anticipating unusual happenings, I don't pay attention to the red flags.

Later, I remembered the overgrown foliage in the front of the house, the broken sidewalk where the bricks had erupted into sharp little mountains. Where the rest of the street's lawns were clipped and immaculately tended, with flat cement sidewalks before each home, Pam's was touched with decay and violence. I know that someone, or something, haunted that house. It succeeded in haunting me.

* * * * *

A few years ago, my daughter Victoria and I vacationed in Victoria, British Columbia. One day we were wandering around Antique Row, an informal designation for several blocks of antique shops, when we spotted an old house that looked interesting — cupola on top, big bay windows, a large front porch. The sign in front said "Antiques," so we climbed the stairs to the front door. There were no other visitors near the house nor on that slice of street; it was as if a wall of silence surrounded the house. All the hanging baskets held dead flowers, clearly an omen if I had been paying attention. No one answered our knock at first, and just as we were about to leave, a man opened the door. He was sullen, unsmiling, not like a person wanting to sell antiques to potential customers. He allowed us in, however, and we wandered through the several rooms on the main floor, clearly parlors and a dining area, overfull with tables and chairs and settees, so close together you could hardly navigate around them. The odd thing was that despite the large windows, the place was dark. I climbed the stairwell to the upper floor. Another series of small rooms, probably originally bedrooms and sitting rooms, also stuffed with furniture, mainly Victorian, with dark carved wood frames and stiff seats. But the deeper I moved into the house, the more foreboding it became. I felt suffocated, claustrophobic, anxious. The house was silent, but alive with some kind of energy I could feel. Something hovered around me, an oppressive feeling like an enveloping cloud. I say, without apology, that it was evil.

I looked around for Victoria, all sorts of thoughts rattling in my head. Where was she? Was she all right? Where was the man who let us in? I stumbled down the stairs as fast as I could, calling her name in a higher than normal voice. With relief, I saw her by the front door, an abstracted look on her face. Our eyes met, and without a word I grabbed the doorknob, turned it, and we hurried out of the house. We went down the stairs quickly and raced up the street. I held tight to her arm all the way up the block, relieved to be out of that house and back in the bright sunshine.

"Something awful happened in that house once," she said. "I think we were lucky to get out."

Maria B. Murad is a writer in Apple Valley, Minnesota. She has published a children's book, short stories, and memoirs and is currently finishing her first novel. She is married with five grown children and three wonderful grandchildren, several of whom show signs of having the Irish Second Sight. Besides writing, she loves to travel (she was in Italy on 9/11). A former ballet dancer, she continues to take classes for the sheer joy of dancing.

Full House

Charles Chupp

"How'd it go this week?" I greeted Jim as I got out of my car. It was nearing sundown and he was loading carpentry tools into his pickup truck. I was puzzled as to why he was taking early departure. The deadline for wrapping up the job was close at hand and very, very important. My retirement was thirty days away, with the closing of our home sale set the week following that.

"We're almost through inside," Jim said. "Got the floors down and the drywall is taped and bedded. We're ahead of schedule."

"I was kinda worried," I admitted. "Last time we talked you said you'd be working nights. I was surprised to see you loading up and getting ready to go."

"I'm not working past sundown anymore," Jim said. "Just in daylight from here on!"

"Why's that?"

"You're not going to believe me," Jim said, "but two nights back we worked until eleven o'clock and something happened to me that's never happened before. There are spooks around this house at night."

I smiled and waited for the punch line. There was none. Jim went into the house for another load of hand tools, and I waited impatiently for him to return. When he did, his helper, Wayne, was with him, sniffing the air with keen interest.

"They're not here yet. Let's get out of here until daylight."

Darkness was descending, but I put my foot on the pickup running board and waited for an explanation. They weren't escaping until one was provided.

Jim and Wayne were both solidly built young men and didn't appear to be prone to hysteria, but they hurried through their account of the last two nights.

As they were loading their tools they detected a sweet-smelling fragrance that they identified later as lilac. Jim said that his grandmother had preferred lilac talcum during her life and his boyhood, so he recognized the smell.

Both men detected the aroma, and although they peered in both directions toward the dimly glowing streetlights they did not see anything or anyone moving. There was no hint of a breeze to waft the faint scent. They laughed and joked nervously on their journey home.

The next night, however, brought affirmation of the first. The lilac scent was back and was accompanied by yet another alarming odor. The newcomer reeked of tobacco — chewing tobacco apparently, since there was no glow of fire.

"The hair on the back of my neck stood straight out," Jim said. "There were two definite spirits or ghosts standing beside us, but they were invisible and didn't make a sound."

"They didn't have to," Wayne added. "I've never believed in spooks — but now I do. If they had gotten in the pickup I would have walked home!"

"Today, one of the locals stopped by to check out how we were doing, and in the course of the conversation he showed us where a man was murdered in the room where we're installing the bath. He was shot dead right where the tub will be located."

"Who shot him?"

"His son-in-law. He and his wife had a fight and the girl had come home to get away from him. She was back in the kitchen with her mama when her husband kicked in the front door.

"The father had a pistol, and so did the son-in-law. They both got shots off, but the son-in-law was only wounded. The old man was declared dead by the Justice of the Peace. The son-in-law went to prison, the mother died within the year, and the daughter left the area. Didn't leave a forwarding address."

"Who told you all that?" I asked.

"I don't remember his name," Jim admitted, "and I didn't ask the names of any of the people who were involved, but I believe he called the father Peanut. It happened about thirty years ago, and this has been rent property ever since. Nobody stays for very long according to the guy who told us the story. We've gotta go. If you'll come back by in the morning we'll give you a guided tour of the progress."

"Don't mention any of this to my wife," I said as they pulled away. "She might have second thoughts about living in this house."

"I wouldn't live here if you gave it to me!" Wayne said. "It will be a beautiful house, but I'm not sure it can be a home."

I stood beside my car for perhaps five minutes, alert for the scent of lilac or tobacco, but my nerve failed me and I didn't enter the house for an inspection tour.

Jim finished the project on time by working weekends, and neither he nor Wayne mentioned the incident again. They wished us good fortune and we moved into the restored house in June of 1985.

Our daughter, Tracy, and her husband, Steve, came for a visit in August. They adored the old house, the big lot, and majestic pecan and sycamore trees. Jokingly, they suggested we will the place to them.

My wife, Margaret, Steve, and I were out in the yard when we heard Tracy scream in terror. Naturally we ran for the door with Steve leading the way. Tracy exited the door with her bathrobe billowing as she ran to Steve and began sobbing in fear.

"A man is groaning in that bathroom!" she said. "Or else he's under the floor! He sounds like he's dying!"

Steve inspected the cavity that always exists beneath pier and beam floor construction and found nothing amiss, but he speculated that some of the newly installed plumbing probably groaned in protest at its positioning and accounted for the noise that Tracy had heard. She was somewhat comforted, but not wholly convinced, and to this date has not showered in our house without someone being present in an adjoining room.

Feeling that the time had come for full disclosure on the history of our old house, I confessed the information that had been passed on to me by the renovators and passersby.

"I've known all along that this place was haunted," Margaret said. "I've seen glows in our bedroom that are not natural. Balls of dim illumination have appeared more than once. Somehow, they don't scare me, but I've never told you," she added. "I was not sure you'd believe me. Ace, our son, saw them one night when he slept over, and someone sat down on the bed, but no one besides Jim has smelled lilacs or tobacco."

I was surprised at the outpouring of testimony concerning unexplainable incidents of course, and wondered why I'd been the only one who somehow possessed immunity.

Margaret's theory is that my hearing is not keen and my sense of smell has been dulled by a lifetime of smoking tobacco. Plus, cynicism is a dominant gene in my makeup.

"Toothaches and electrical shocks can't be seen," Steve observed, "but there's no doubt in the mind of the person who's experienced them as to their existence."

We've accepted the probability of watchers in our old house, and have not put the place up for sale.

Charles Chupp is a second-generation Texan of 1929 vintage, with a first wife who has lasted better than half a century. They have collaborated on two offspring — one of each variety. He became addicted to writing back in 1952 and has not been able to break the habit. Charles has written for many Texas newspapers and magazines — some of which he recalls quite well and others he can't remember. Some of those publications are still in business, but he claims no credit for their success. Similarly, he shoulders no blame for those who didn't make it. He's published and marketed two books and had two serialized in *Messenger* magazine, and has produced a weekly column for the last twenty years. Charles has a web site that may be marveled over at www.charleschupp.com.

A Personal True Encounter

Jean C. Fisher

My very first psychic experience happened when I was about seven, while sitting at the kitchen table writing a letter to "Nanny," my paternal grandmother, who had been ill for about a year by that time.

Years earlier, Nanny had taken care of me while my mother was caring for my dying father in the hospital. He was her "favorite" child and I was his only offspring (even though he had been married more than once). Nanny was born the 11th of March, and I, the 10th, so she always told everyone that I was her "birthday present." We were very close.

As I sat by myself with paper and pencil, I remember that I had written, in clumsy block letters at the top of the page, "DEAR NANNY." At that point, I guess I lapsed into a kind of trance. I remember trying to move my head and hands, but I was unable to. It was as if my body were frozen. In a moment, a figure that appeared to be my Nanny just materialized out of thin air and seemed to be floating about five feet off the floor in front of me. While I could make out the shape of her body, it was as if it was made of a material that I could see through. I tried to move my head up to look into her eyes, but was still frozen where I sat and could not!

Nanny began "speaking" to me, although it was more like I heard her voice in my head rather than heard it with my ears. She spoke to me for what seemed like a very long time. She told me that she loved me very much, and that I would be told that she had died but that I was not to cry or be upset about it because she was in a wonderful place. She told me she was not in pain anymore and that she had reunited with my (deceased) father and that she was very, very happy.

She also told me that, in the years to come, she would always be near me, watching over me, so I was not to miss her because she would still be with me. Then the figure of Nanny dissolved completely and I was able to move once again.

I dashed into the living room and told my mother that I had "seen" Nanny, but she dismissed me, saying something like, "That's nice, dear," and went on reading her newspaper.

The next morning my mother received a phone call and she told me, in a very serious tone, that my Nanny had passed away in the night. As she told me this, she was looking at me intently, I suppose in order to judge my reaction. I told her that I knew because Nanny had told me all about it the night before, when I saw her in the kitchen.

Over the next several weeks, my mother broached the subject of my grandmother's death with me many times, trying, she said, to make me understand that Nanny was gone forever and that it was okay for me to be sad and cry about it. Of course, I did not cry, because my Nanny had specifically instructed me not to do so!

Finally, in desperation, my mother took me to a child psychologist to find out why this daughter of hers, who had been so very close to her grandmother, was not showing any outward signs of grief about her passing. My mother insisted it simply was not normal!

After a few sessions with the psychologist, he told her it seemed as though I had had a great deal of emotional attachment to my grandmother. Additionally, I seemed to understand the concept of death, and that my grandmother was dead. Baffled himself by my apparent lack of outward signs of grief, he said it could stem from a profound spiritual or religious belief in the afterlife nurtured in me by those around me. My mother, an avowed atheist, pooh-poohed his theory and ended my sessions with him soon thereafter.

That was my first encounter with "seeing dead people." However, I have had many more such experiences in my forty or so subsequent years of life. I suppose the reason I find these apparitions neither frightening nor distressing is because my first encounter was with a person I loved so very, very much — my Nanny.

Jean C. Fisher lives in Northern California, where she does freelance writing, volunteers her time at Luther Burbank's Gold Ridge Farm, and serves as a co-president of the Western Sonoma County Historical Society.

Love Lingers

Peggye Swenson

In the 1960s we lived in a mansion in Denver. I'm not kidding. A mansion, yes, but standing on the threshold of being razed. It towered over the street like a gigantic gray spider offering safety within its walls. I loved that old limestone house and every inch of the indoors that gave my children a place to play without being threatened by traffic.

My husband worked one shift, I another. We had a live-in babysitter, Nola, for the kids (eight of them) and more than plenty of room for all. It was a magic time.

Since I worked 10 P.M. to 6 A.M., I left after the children were in bed, always making sure all doors were locked before turning my back on the house. Nola was a nervous sort, so I made sure everything she might need in the night was at hand. When she told me about someone passing her door in the wee hours of the morning, I wasn't concerned. It was either one of the kids on the way to the bathroom or one of us getting home from work. She didn't press the point and neither did I, but I did notice that after dark she seldom left her room.

A week or so later my oldest daughter, Penny, who was ten, asked a question that chilled me to the bone. "Who is that man who comes into our room to look out the window?" She shared a bedroom at the back of the second floor with her seven-year-old sister, Kathy.

"What man?" I glanced at Nola who returned my glance with icy silence.

"He comes into the room, goes to the window and looks out. Then he says 'no' and runs away." Penny's curious eyes peered into mine. As far as she was concerned, Mother knew all the answers.

But I didn't know this one. I had a suspicion that Nola entertained a young man while we were out of the house, but if she did, she wasn't about to 'fess up. I decided to wait. The "strange man" might be a figment of Penny's overactive imagination.

A couple of nights later I got sick at work. The shift was well covered so I went home. The house was dark, save for a night-light on the stairs, looming overhead in a protective manner. I unlocked the front door, relocking it after I was inside, dropped my coat and purse on a chair, and turned to the stairs. As I started up the broad staircase a swirl of movement at the top landing caught my attention. I continued going up when a man in an opera cape appeared above me, rushing toward me. I shouted something like "who are you" or "what are you doing in my house" as he plunged down the stairs toward me. We were about to collide and I threw up my hands in protection and he ran right through me. Totally shocked I clung to the banister as he continued down the stairs and out the front door — without opening it.

My legs were shaking so hard I could barely stand. As I slid down to sit on a step, Penny appeared at the top of the stairs. "Did you see him? I followed him when he left my room."

She sat beside me on the stairs and I grilled her about the person. She told me what I'd seen, except her take on the opera cloak was "a Batman cape, but it isn't red."

If I'd heard her description before my encounter with what I now believed was an apparition, I would have discounted it. Batman was a hit and my kids were big fans. The inclusion of a Batman cape would have assured me Penny was dreaming. But I had seen him — had him run right through me on the stairs. I knew he wasn't flesh and blood. I needed time to think. Just to be sure, I moved the girls' room from one end of the hall to the other, leaving their previous bedroom empty. Although I suggested Nola might like that room best, she turned wide, frightened eyes on me and shook her head. I didn't press the point.

In the next few days I took the opportunity to check into the old house. The real estate agent didn't know anything about its history, except that it had been built as a wedding present by one of the strike-it-rich miners for his bride. The agent had the year and the cost of the original structure and that was all.

With the year in hand, I went to the historical society to see what I could discover about the house. I waded through yellowed pages of purchases of lumber, stone, marble, and labor with no answers. Checking into newspaper records, I found an old engraving of the finished product with the announcement of the upcoming marriage of Simon J. Templeton and Miss Penelope Andrews, stating a festive gala was planned for February 14th — Valentine's Day. The pictures of the engaged couple appeared as part of the story, and I knew the instant I saw Templeton's face that he was my ghost. For ghost he was. The wedding had been planned for a full century past.

I scanned the next few issues of the newspaper and found what I was looking for in the February 15th issue. A tragic accident had put an end to the Templeton-Andrews wedding plans. While coming into town in a sleigh, the bride-elect had been killed when the vehicle overturned and she was struck in the head by a runner. According to the reporter, Templeton had been watching for his bride from a window in his house and witnessed the entire event, totally unable to stop or alter what had happened.

I knew who our ghosts were and carefully explained to my daughters that the man would not hurt them — he was locked in a moment in time, condemned to repeat it.

For myself, I wondered why no one had ever seen him before. There were no hints of a haunting from other people who had lived in the house, no reports of a haunting that may have seemed the continuation of a love story.

When the house was pulled down some months later, I wondered what had happened to our star-crossed lovers. Repeating the instant all hope ended must have been hell for Templeton.

Peggye Swenson is a retired award-winning reporter/photographer. As a staff writer for *Front Page* and *Inside* detective magazines in the '50s, she cut her teeth on police investigations with the Los Angeles Police Department. She's a member of Freelance Writers' Network of Fort Worth (Texas) and a 20-year member of Texas Press Women.

Death Message

Peggye Swenson

I was on a train from Los Angeles to Wichita Falls, Texas, one dark night in 1952. Weighed down with diaper bag, overnight case, and three-month-old daughter, I was too tired to sleep. The movement of the train was calming to my child, who snored peacefully.

My mind was too busy with what I would say to my father when I arrived at my destination. We'd been estranged for more than two years and my leave-taking hadn't been calm or pleasant. I had a great deal to apologize for and the night seemed perfect for searching out the right words to share.

The windows acted as a mirror, backed by black landscape. I could see travelers sleeping in their seats and the passing of others headed up or down the aisle.

Penny stirred in her sleep, capturing my attention as I felt someone slide into the empty seat beside me.

"You're too late," he said.

I glanced up at the window and realized there was no one sitting next to me.

I turned to look at the seat. It looked like the weight of a person pressed on the seat cushion, but he or she wasn't visible. That gave me something else to think about. Just in case, I checked my watch. It was 2:50 Pacific Time, which made it 4:50 at my destination.

Not knowing what difference it made, I closed my eyes and dismissed the visitor. I must have been dreaming out loud.

The train chugged into El Paso at six that morning. Penny was awake and loudly demanding food while I tried to make our seating arrangement more comfortable. I still had hours to go before we arrived.

There was some bustle with people getting off and others getting on at the depot. I hoped my little nest wouldn't be invaded by someone needing a seat.

The conductor stopped at my seat, read from a piece of paper in his hands, and asked my name. Not understanding why he wanted to know, I answered. I'd never been on a train before and had no idea the procedure of travel.

When I shared my name, he snapped to attention and informed me he had a telegram awaiting me at the depot desk. That put me in a quandary. In Los Angeles I'd had help with bags and baby getting on the train. At the end of my journey there'd also be someone to help. The thought of trying to drag all this stuff off the train boggled my mind.

The conductor recognized my confusion. "I'll wait here with the baby if you want to skip off the train and get your message."

He was a sweetheart. I had never received a telegram before and added it to the list of firsts I was experiencing. Although I felt a tinge of excitement, it was edged in black. It had to be bad news. Although I had dismissed the nighttime words, I hadn't forgotten them.

Suddenly I was swept into a whirlwind of activity. The telegrapher had alerted local police, who were waiting for me. Without sharing anything, my bags, baby, and I were gathered from the train, pushed into the rear of a patrol car, and driven to what seemed the middle of nowhere. In an open field an airplane sat, engines running.

Once on board I had the first chance to read the telegram. "He's gone. Dad died at four-fifty this morning. Vic." I wadded the yellow sheet and stuck it in my pocket as the plane took off, headed I knew not where.

I don't remember my first airplane flight. I don't recall anything about the train trip other than the black night where windows became mirrors. I do remember the words. "You're too late."

All the things I wanted to tell my dad weren't wasted. Somehow I knew he understood.

Peggye Swenson is a retired award-winning reporter/photographer. As a staff writer for *Front Page* and *Inside* detective magazines in the '50s, she cut her teeth on police investigations with the Los Angeles Police Department. She's a member of Freelance Writers' Network of Fort Worth (Texas) and a 20-year member of Texas Press Women.

"Mein Gott! Du hast einen Geist gefangen!"

Bill R. Cannon

"My God! You've captured a ghost!" These were the words I exclaimed to Marianne, my Berlin-born wife, when I picked up the photos of our honeymoon trip in Germany in the spring of 1980.

After spending several days with family and friends in what was then West Berlin, my new bride and I had continued on by car to south Germany for a long-awaited visit with friends near Lake Konstanz. As we rounded a curve in the beautiful German countryside near the town of Bingen on the Rhein River, we were greeted by a billboard reading "Spend a night in a German castle!" One does not travel the Rhein between Bingen and Koblenz without thinking about the legends of knights and robbers and their fortresses and castles. In this region, the Rhein is sprinkled with some of Germany's most historic castles. Around every bend of the famous waterway lies a castle, each one more intriguing than the last. What a romantic and memorable experience it would be, I thought, to spend one night of our honeymoon in a centuries-old residence of a Teutonic knight, or a wealthy German landholder at least. My Berliner bride agreed, and we swung our borrowed Mercedes left along the river in the direction of Koblenz. Neither of us felt the slightest bit of angst about spending a night in an ancient castle whose occupants had been dead for centuries. A passenger train was winding its way past the numerous Rheinland vineyards on the opposite bank of the river as boats of various sizes plied the river's waters as they had for generations. The castle advertised on the billboard was Schloss Reichenstein in Trechlingshausen am Rhein. This was one of the region's largest castles, and had a thousand-year-old history, which included, along with its neighboring castle, use as a nest for some of the Rhein's most vicious robber-knights! One resident, Gerhard of Rheinbodo (1151-1156), raged as a robber-knight through the region and demanded goods violently from travelers and shipmen. In 1213 he was disposed of. To the great relief of a lot of people, I'm sure.

We could see how this medieval castle would be a formidable fortress to conquer — its main tower with its crenellations rose skyward out of solid rock cliffs. Marianne and I were both impressed with the construction of such a fortress erected so long ago of solid stone walls that were at least two feet thick. With some of the castle in ruins, we were able to better inspect its construction. We were also impressed with our room. While not lavishly appointed, it was furnished with dated but comfortable furniture, including, surprisingly enough, a small black and white TV. The large window furnished us an unobstructed view of the Rhein and a portion of the town of Trechlingshausen. The only real reminder that we were in a medieval castle was the abnormal height of the ceilings. This was most noticeable in the long hall that knifed through the castle, giving access to other rooms and the castle's common bathroom, as well as the stairs leading to the dining room where we were to dine on our complimentary breakfast. Reichenstein castle was home to an excellent medieval museum based on the castle's history. Walking down the long hall, my wife and I both experienced the same old cliché expression of wonderment: "Boy, if these old walls could talk!" After one sees the suits of body armor and centuries-old weaponry, both personal weapons of defense and medieval troop armament, as well as table settings and candleholders used by the castle's occupants long before America was discovered, it gave us plenty to imagine about life in the castle in centuries past.

Walking back from breakfast on the morning of our departure, as I entered the seemingly endless hallway with its hunting trophies hanging from the walls, I saw an ornately carved straight-back chair with a regal-looking brocade back and seat covering near the end of the dimly lit hall. The wooden chair had an extremely tall back and looked, I thought, more like a throne, but slimmer. I thought a photo of me in this regal setting would not only be a good souvenir, but would also accurately display the abnormal height of the castle's ceilings. I assumed a dignified posture in the chair, directly under a mounted stag's head. Marianne attempted to stifle a giggle as she focused on this Texas tourist trying so hard to look proper in these ancient surroundings. As the flash filled the big hall, which was in semi-darkness, I wondered again about what life must have been like when the castle was occupied and alive with activity.

I didn't know it at the time, but Marianne and I might not have been the only persons in that long, dimly lit hall that morning in Schloss Reichenstein! For when I went to pick up the envelope containing our honeymoon pictures from Germany, my heart skipped a beat as I came to that memento of our stay in the castle. There I sat, posing stiffly in the antique chair that once belonged to the nobility that made Schloss Reichenstein their home. What took my breath was that some thing, or someone, was there with me! Something was in the photograph that certainly wasn't seen by Marianne or me that morning we checked out of the castle and made our way to Konstanz. Hanging, or more accurately hovering, above my head was an almost shapeless wispy form that resembled paintings I had seen of the American Indian's shaman found painted in caves. The form did not appear solid and was not opaque. It was a transparent white in color and filmy. I immediately called Marianne and said, "You captured a ghost in your photo of me at Schloss Reichenstein!"

This photo was shown to numerous friends, each of whom had his or her own idea as to the nature of the ethereal apparition in the photo. Everything from "a reflection from a wall mirror we had not noticed" to "the light bouncing off the antlers of the mounted stag head." But what, I ask you, if it is the spirit of a member of the castle household who took umbrage at this uninvited guest (a foreigner, at that!) sitting in his or her favorite chair? I shall always treasure not only the night Marianne and I spent in this bit of ancient German history, but also what might have been my personal visit from a robber-knight out of the medieval past. The ancient ghost, if it was a ghost, didn't manifest itself in any way other than its appearance during my sitting for the castle portrait. Had it done so, I am not ashamed to admit, we might have checked out earlier!

Author and historian Bill R. Cannon is a native Texan. Born in Temple in 1930, he moved with his family to Dallas in 1935. He has lived in Dallas County for nearly 70 years. He began his writing career in 1987 after a paralyzing stroke forced him to sell his industrial security and investigations company. Being forced into retirement gave him the opportunity to try his hand at serious writing. Having a deep love for Texas, and inspired by his mother's stories of growing up in Texas in the late 1800s, he began to preserve on paper some of the unusual facts she related to him as a child. Sure that as vast and diverse as Texas is there must be many such anecdotal stories, he used his now free time and his investigative experience to research the state's history and cultures. The result was a collection of little-known and forgotten facts and legends about Texas, which he calls Texas trivia. He assembled these trivia items into categories, which became his first book, *A Treasury of Texas Trivia*, published in 1997 by Republic of Texas Press. For several years Mr. Cannon wrote a weekly Texas trivia column for a Dallas-Fort Worth area newspaper. Mr. Cannon can be heard daily at 6:20 A.M. on radio station KAAM 770 AM where he provides a Texas trivia question to be answered by listeners. Mr. Cannon has also written *A Treasury of Texas Trivia II*, *Treasury of Texas Humor*, and *Tales from Toadsuck, Texas*. His most recent book is *Texas, Land of Legend and Lore*.

Grandmother's Rocking Chair

Virginiae Blackmon

The last orange glow of the summer sunset silhouetted the figure of a woman rocking rhythmically in the cane-backed chair on the front porch. Grandmother vowed to stay in the farmhouse where she was born and died. And, for a while, she did.

Built in 1898 by Grandmother's parents, the white clapboard house, shaded by two giant oak trees, was well-loved and, for a long time, kept in good repair. It nestled peacefully among crepe myrtle trees they planted, at the edge of a cotton field near a farm road into Springtown, Texas. My mom and her brothers and sisters grew up here.

Every member of the family worked hard to farm the fifteen acres, take care of the cows and chickens, and tend Grandmother's pride and joy, the quarter-acre vegetable garden. She maintained a daily ritual of visiting the garden, especially during growing season. After supper while Grandpa supervised the children doing dishes, she went to the garden to thank God for all the good food to feed the family. This gave her a few much-needed minutes to herself.

Sometimes Grandpa accompanied her. I remember stories about the kids peeking through the window curtains to watch them. Grandpa often picked up a handful of the rich black earth, smelled it, then tossed it up for the wind to scatter. They held hands like new lovers and talked. The kids giggled and made remarks among themselves while witnessing Grandpa put his strong arms around Grandmother for a hug and a kiss.

Grandmother gathered the vegetables, washing them at the pump next to the back porch. She wet a clean white feed sack with the cool water and put it over the dishpan full of vegetables. After seating herself on the front porch in the cane-backed rocking chair, she would pull off her bonnet and remove the hairpins, letting her dark brown hair fall around her shoulders. Then she would slowly wipe her brow and hands, enjoying the cool cloth. She rocked in silence, head resting against the tall chair back, watching the sunset, surveying her treasures (as she called them). Continuing to rock, she began to snap peas, shuck corn, skin onions, or wipe tomatoes with a dry cloth.

She and Grandpa chose this time to figure the surplus. Chores, done well by the children over the past week without too much encouragement, were rewarded with money made by selling vegetables, eggs, butter, and cream at the market in town on Saturday.

In seasons the temperature did not permit sitting on the front porch, Grandpa moved her chair in by the fireplace where she could watch the sunset through the west window. Times there were no vegetables to pick and the garden rested for spring, to quote Grandmother, she darned socks or pieced quilts, but never until she had rested in silence and watched the sunset. On cloudy days she said God hid the sunset today so she could appreciate it more in a day or so.

After her rest time, she might take more than one child in her lap, sing with the children, tell them stories, or teach Bible verses. There was always laughter and fun in the little board house in the cotton field, and those who lived there through the years thrived.

After Grandpa died, Grandmother stayed on alone in her beloved farmhouse, surrounded by her memories. Different family members, mostly grandchildren, visited regularly to help with upkeep.

The garden no longer covered a quarter-acre. But Grandmother insisted on growing some things such as okra, squash, tomatoes, and onions. A few plants replaced rows of everything. She had five peach trees providing two varieties of peaches that ripened in early summer and late summer. She no longer canned her harvest. As Grandmother used to say, she "stored" everything in the big freezer. She also "stored" cookies, cakes, etc., and was generous with her family and neighbors. Children and grandchildren got together on her seventy-seventh birthday and gave her the large freezer, which had to occupy one corner of a bedroom, next to the electric clothes dryer.

Even though her chores kept her inside more, she still enjoyed her garden and the ritual of rocking on the front porch or by the fireplace to enjoy the sunset.

Grandmother died early in the fall of 1982, just after sunset, in her bed in the farmhouse she dearly loved. After the church service and burial beside her kin in the nearby cemetery, the family and several friends gathered at the farmhouse. We were surprised to find a large sheet cake, baked two weeks before, "stored" in the freezer marked "for my wake." It was yellow cake with lemon hard sauce icing, a favorite of every one who knew her.

I was sitting on the edge of the front porch enjoying my cake, watching Grandmother's sunset, when her chair began to rock. There was no wind and no one had touched the chair out of respect for her. The motion continued until the sun had settled behind the horizon, then stopped. Some tried to rationalize what had happened, but I saw it and definitely felt her presence.

The next day I went back to the house to enjoy her things — and yes, to have another piece of yellow cake with the scrumptious icing. I cut a generous piece, poured a glass of milk, and settled on the edge of the porch. I wanted to see if Grandmother would sit with me. Just before sunset, the chair began to rock. As the last glow of orange and crimson illuminated the west end of the porch, I saw clearly the outline of Grandmother, her loose shoulder-length hair, bonnet in her lap, her smiling face gazing toward the horizon. Then she turned, looked straight at me, and spoke. "Your mom and all the brothers and sisters are together now up here. Heaven is such a fun place for your babies and your mother enjoys them so. Grandpa says it's okay for me to come back to visit my house a while and I will." As the darkness grew deeper, her form faded and the chair was still.

About two weeks later, a couple approached the family and asked to buy the property. We planned to meet one evening to go over what the family expected concerning the sale. Grandmother's chair was moved from the porch to the front room by the fireplace. The curtains on the west window were pushed back. On the floor close to the chair I placed a small sewing basket of quilt pieces she had worked on in the weeks before her passing. The room was warm and cozy, filled with sweet smells from burning pecan wood. The time was chosen to show the house in anticipation of Grandmother's visit.

The couple arrived about an hour before sunset. We walked the property and examined the old clapboard-covered barn. They were delighted to realize the logs of the original structure could be seen from the inside, sturdy and still in place. They asked if the boards could be removed to restore the old barn. I told them we would ask Grandmother.

As sunset approached we sat in the front room. I served yellow cake and listened to the story of the first time my Grandmother had served her famous cake. Just before sunset she joined us. The sewing basket moved a few inches, and the chair turned slightly more toward the west window, then began to rock. I watched my friends, not knowing what to expect from them. Grandmother had been gone — well, she wasn't gone obviously — but she had died a few weeks ago. My friends smiled but were very quiet.

We discussed the conditions of the sale. Only once was Grandmother still. It was when the couple asked about the chair — if they purchased the house with some of the furnishings, was it included? Grandmother had specifically stated in her will that the rocker was to remain with the house as long as she did, then given to her sister's only daughter. The couple agreed. The rocking began again and lasted quite a while that night. The property sold and our friends moved in to enjoy retirement in the country. For almost three months the rocking continued. The chair was placed in the precise spot on the west end of the porch for the summer, then moved to the front room by the fireplace as the weather began to change.

I was invited to supper one cold November evening. Nothing much had changed. The remaining pieces of furniture were exactly as Grandmother had left them except a new queen-sized bed had been added to the main bedroom. Grandmother's bed was now in the guestroom.

We sat in the front room and talked and enjoyed the warmth of the fire.

"I hope no one minds me moving her bed," the lady said. "I am not bothered she died in the bed; I just felt as though I was intruding in a very private place and found this quite undignified. Do you think she understands?"

Though it was long after sunset, the chair began to rock. We knew she approved.

About four months after her death, the rocking stopped. My friend called me one evening, saying the chair had not moved for a week. I visited in the evening for three days, watching and waiting. We even made yellow cake to eat at sunset but she did not visit. The chair never rocked again and was passed on to the designated heir.

A year passed. The man had a heart attack and they moved to town on the advice of his physician. They sold the property to the man that owned the adjoining acreage.

Two years later a friend and I drove to the "old homeplace" for an afternoon picnic. The house, now used to store hay, was in severe disrepair, the chimney falling down. Orb weaver spiders decorated the inside doorways with large webs of delicate designs. With a piece of the famous cake each, we sat on the edge of the porch and I told her stories of Grandmother rocking on the porch and by the fireplace and the visits I remembered as a young child.

Now only the barn remains, the clapboards still covering the original log structure. In my garage are two boards from the blue painted front room ceiling of the house (for picture frames), four bricks from the chimney, and the vividly remembered sunset silhouette of Grandmother rocking on the porch in the cane-backed chair Grandpa made for her as a wedding present.

Dr. Virginiae Blackmon is an author, photojournalist/traveler, lecturer, exhibiting artist, spinner, and weaver. She has published articles on botany and scanning electron microscopy for science journals, medical articles for reference books, and has written for regional newsletters and national magazines on spinning and weaving. Her expertise is in the fields of journalism (news reporting), photography (journalism and art), medicine, botany, general science, travel, and fiber arts.

That Old House And Its Occupants

Helen D. Kennedy

"Okay, so the house is sixty-five years old."

"Does that mean it's haunted?"

I never believed in haunted houses, even when my mother came to visit and complained of noises upstairs. I used to tell her that the house was old and the noise was just the house settling.

The house had originally been a barn and had been owned by two old gentlemen who kept their horses there and had a small farm area. That section of town had at one time been country. The barn was the only thing standing for miles around and I am told the old gentlemen fought constantly and often came near to blows.

As the years went by, the property was sold and the barn became a house, with the hayloft becoming two bedrooms upstairs. A kitchen, bath, and living room had been added to the downstairs before I bought it. I added a bedroom in front of the living room. I was always very comfortable in that house and the creaking noises never bothered me.

I do confess to a bit of a fright when I heard what I thought was footsteps going upstairs one night. They were very slow and laboring. I did run next door and had my neighbor come over and check things out. I felt very foolish when he found nothing and I vowed then not to let my imagination run away with me again. I really didn't believe in ghosts.

Then one evening I had settled in bed for the night when a nagging, uneasy feeling came over me and it seemed as if someone were in the house. I knew there was no one else there. I had checked the windows that had been open during the day and the doors to make sure that all was locked. I reminded myself that everything was secure.

As I turned my face towards the living room, I could look into the kitchen and see the refrigerator. All of a sudden I saw two figures there who appeared to be having a heated argument. I could not hear their words — they were inaudible — but somehow I knew they were shouting at each other. One of the men was flailing his hands about and the other just stood there shaking his head. The figures had no distinguishable characteristics but I sensed they were two male figures.

Now, absolute panic overtook me and I did not know what to do except to lie there very still and try not to make a sound. I did not know if they were going to rob me, perhaps kill me, or who knows what.

I was so scared that I dared not move. I lay there afraid to breathe for fear they would hear me. My heart was beating so loud that I could hear it, and I was afraid they would hear it as well. I slowly eased myself onto my back and closed my eyes. After what seemed like an hour, I squinted and slowly turned my head towards the kitchen again. The shadowy figures were still there as they continued their argument. The figures had shape but no depth or color, only an opaque grayish hue.

By this time, fear and imagination had really taken hold. I once again tried to close my eyes. I had planned that I would keep my eyes closed and feign sleep if they came into the room. I lay there waiting for what seemed like hours. Every so often I would sneak a look. They were still there. The fear became more than I could bear. My heart was racing, quiet breathing became more and more impossible, and I must have mercifully passed out.

The next morning when I awoke, I remembered the night before. Daylight made things seem a lot different. I knew I had experienced something very strange, something I did not understand. I got out of bed and looked around. Everything was in order except the rug in front of the refrigerator had the appearance of a struggle and was crumpled. It looked as if someone had been shifting his feet on it. I knew it was not in that condition when I went to bed.

I have been accused of being asleep and dreaming all those things. No, I was definitely not asleep. I had been lying there thinking of all the things I had to do the next day, and nothing was bothering me before I became aware of these beings.

Were these two figures (I will call them spirits) arguing over me? If not, why were they in my house? Was one a dark spirit, there to do me harm, and the other there to protect me? I have never been so frightened in all my life. I know now that "another dimension" exists and I find it scary.

The memory of that night stayed with me and I told one of my neighbors whose house had been one of the first built on that block. She knew the two old gentlemen who had lived there. She laughed and said, "You have just met the old farmers who owned your house when it was a barn. I am not surprised that they were arguing; they always did that." She related how one always threw his arms around and the other just stood there shaking his head. This was exactly what I had seen the figures in front of the refrigerator do.

Was it really the two farmers having their usual fight? Or was it, as I had thought, a dark spirit and a protective spirit having an argument over me? I will never know.

Thankfully the apparitions never appeared again as long as I lived in the house. The creaks remained but, after all, the house was old and was still settling. I did remove the rug from in front of the refrigerator, in case they came again, so I wouldn't have to see it crumpled the next morning. And just in case, I whispered a soft thanks to my protector.

Helen Kennedy now resides in Florida, although her first love is California, where she resided for twenty-five years and still calls home. She has been a vocalist, model, and actress but willingly declares that writing gives her the most satisfaction.

As an editor for the Owensboro Symphony Orchestra newsletter, she wrote about visiting artists who performed with the symphony, not all of whom were musicians; there were various acts as well as a politician or two for good measure. Helen has written for magazines and even published some poetry. She is now concentrating mostly on travel writing.

Absolution: A Ghost Story

Zaphra Reskakis

It was hot that day in August 1972 as we sat in our living room in our apartment at 97-409 62nd Drive in Rego Park, New York. The temperature in New York had been soaring for days. Even with the air conditioner full blast, I was drenched, as were my twelve-year-old daughter and thirteen-year-old son. We were sitting in the living room watching television. We were sweaty even though we were only wearing light shirts and shorts. Night had crept up suddenly, as it does on midsummer nights, and although it was only nine o'clock, the heat was so oppressive that all three of us were nodding off as the television set droned on. I got up from the easy chair, yawned, and said, "I'm going to take a cold shower and then I'm going to bed. It's just too hot. What about...?"

I stopped in mid-sentence, shivered, and hugged myself for warmth. I felt clammy as the perspiration froze on my body. Suddenly the room had become cold, absolutely frigid and icy. It felt like a crypt. Stunned, I stepped back and fell into my chair. I looked at my children, who also were shivering, and then I seemed to forget that they were there and where I was. Although I saw nothing, I felt a presence and felt a light touch on my shoulder, but I was not afraid. Later, my son and daughter told me that they too had felt the room turn cold, but they neither sensed nor saw everything. My son had checked the air conditioner but the air was no colder than before, yet the room for a few minutes was almost unbearably cold. They told me that I was crying and talking to myself, but they could not understand what I was saying because I was blubbering and talking in Greek.

But I was not talking to myself. I was talking to the presence in the room. It was their Grandfather George, my father-in-law, who had died the past March. My father-in-law was a proud man who loved me. When his son divorced me in 1969 in order to marry his girlfriend of many years, George was distraught and had not gone to his son's wedding. He remained distant to both his son and his son's new wife.

Although my children saw their father and their grandparents, I had minimal contact with my ex-husband and absolutely no contact with his family. In 1971, Grandpa George was diagnosed with terminal cancer and was in the hospital. When I heard this, I was distraught. I wanted to see him, but I knew the man. I had not seen him in two years and if I went to the hospital to see him I was afraid that he might realize that he was critically ill. When he had his first bout with cancer in 1950, the news was kept from him. The family felt he would become despondent and unable to cope. In those years, decisions such as this were common. He had survived both the first illness and a recurrence two years later. With the present diagnosis, both the physician and the family again felt it best to tell him nothing. I wanted to respect their wishes but more than that I did not want to hurt this man whom I dearly loved. I did not go to the hospital. A few months later, when he passed away, I did go to the wake and to his funeral. Although I had paid my respects to the family, I had not seen George while he was alive and had not said goodbye to this man who truly loved me. Even though I felt that I had made the right decision, I felt both angry and guilty and it constantly bothered me. I could not forgive myself.

On this August evening in my ice-cold living room, I did not see my father-in-law, but I felt his presence and I heard him. I sat back in the chair and realized I was no longer shivering although I could still feel the cold. I heard George's voice say, "Zaphra, don't be afraid. It's me." He did not speak to me in English. He spoke in Greek, the language that we usually spoke to one another. I was crying because I was sad and not frightened. As best as I can remember this was our conversation:

I answered, "Oh, dad. I am not afraid but I am so sorry. Please forgive me. I feel so guilty and angry. I should have come to see you in the hospital all those months that you were there. I should have."

"I know you wanted to. But I also know why you didn't come."

"But I should have. So many times I thought about coming when the children were coming to see you."

"I know that, my child. I know that. It was for the best. It would have been painful for both of us if you came. You made the right choice. That is why I am here. I understand why you didn't come. You could not. I know how troubled you have been."

"I am so sorry, Dad."

"My child, you have nothing to be sorry for."

I felt a soft brush on my cheek, and as suddenly as it had become cold it became the same August day of perhaps five minutes ago. I was relieved that George knew why I had not seen him in his last few days here on Earth, and with this realization came peace of mind for me as well.

Zaphra Reskakis, MS. RPh. is a semi-retired clinical pharmacist whose work in progress is a collection of family stories titled *Daughter of Zeus and Hera*. She is the proud *yiayia* ("grandma" in Greek) of Amanda, Brendan, Cory, Nicholas, and Michael who inspired her to write the *yiayia* stories that she has told them. She has been published in *Hellenic Times* (Boston) and in *Chicken Soup for the Nurse's Soul* (2001), *We Remember the Fifties* (*Reminisce*, 2002), *Tactfully Cooking* (2002), and *9-11*, a collection of essays, poems, and stories (Michelle Cherrix, 2002). She has also been published in magazines: *FATE, Reminisce, What's Cooking*, and *Storyteller*, and on the Internet: loseyouridentity, clevermag.com, and Mr. Beller's Neighborhood. Zaphra is a member of The Storytelling Center and Barbara Aliprantis' The Storytelling Exchange and has appeared at Cornelia Street Cafe in Greenwich Village, New York, and The South Street Seaport, New York. She is delighted to be part of this book and wishes the publisher good luck in this venture. She can be e-mailed at yiayiazaph@aol.com.

The Well-Dressed Ghost

Virginiae Blackmon

I have experienced a particular guardian spirit on two occasions, both at my children's elementary school. Each time she saved me from serious bodily harm and each time, as I turned around to thank her, she vanished.

Room Mother is a demanding responsibility but most rewarding. That year I was up against some tough competition. Very talented mothers had held the honored office before me. They made all the gifts for Christmas, Valentine's Day, and Easter, and baked for every occasion. I began with great enthusiasm.

My understanding boss allowed me to take my lunch break at odd hours to deliver home-baked goodies and decorations to school. I perused many magazines and cookbooks for interesting themes for party favors, cake decorations, and new ideas in general. Birthdays were celebrated once a month, although the Room Mother sent a card to each of the thirty-one children on the appropriate day. Children with birthdays in the summer were not left out. A day was chosen to celebrate the summer birthdays. During vacation, the Room Mother sent a card as well. Near the end of March, I prepared party favors, fancily decorated homemade cupcakes, and drinks to celebrate birthdays for the month.

A little late leaving the office that day, I parked on the street at the west end of South High Mount Elementary School in Fort Worth, the entrance nearest my daughter's classroom. There were eighteen wide concrete steps leading up to the building entrance with no handrail, an unsteady climb with arms full.

Getting all the bundles into the classroom required two fast trips up the concrete stairs. Everything needed to be ready before recess ended. What a reward to see the faces light up when the children entered the room.

The party successful, we packed up Tupperware and serving utensils. As I hurried through the exit door to descend the concrete stairway, I tripped on the first step and felt myself jolt forward. With arms spread wide, as bundles dropped and bounced down the stairs, I had a mental flash of my body careening down all that concrete face first. Suddenly a lady in a navy blue suit reached out and with strong arms caught me across the chest and pushed me upright. She held me for a moment before letting go. I caught my breath and continued to the car. She walked beside me, holding my arm and smiling. She helped me gather my things and we put them in the backseat. My heart pounded as I looked back, thinking a fall would surely have caused a serious head injury and several broken bones, if not death. Neither of us spoke.

I leaned against my VW convertible for a moment, then reached to hug her for saving my life. I watched her disappear.

That was the first time I experienced this strange phenomenon. The lady was not an imagined puff of smoke or some floating image. Her grasp was very strong. For several minutes after the incident I felt the pressure across my chest and on my arms where she caught me to prevent the fall. This took an enormous amount of strength.

The next morning I spoke with the principal by phone and asked the identity of the short lady with brown hair wearing a navy blue suit, a pearl necklace, and navy shoes. The principal did not know. She didn't remember any teachers or staff wearing a navy blue suit to school that day and asked if perhaps it could have been one of the mothers. I knew most of the mothers by sight if not by name and I didn't recognize her. The lady did not drive away — I would have seen her. She just disappeared.

She must be a guardian spirit; at least that is what I chose to call her.

The second incident took place at the same school on carnival night. I was hanging a string of colored lights in a tree over one of the booths. The ladder sat unevenly on the ground. I felt it wobble as I climbed up to the top step to fasten the last light, steadying myself by holding a tree limb. Two of us had come to finish setting up and the other mother had gone inside. I was alone on the playground, down below the wide patio at the back of school and out of sight.

The ladder wobbled again. As it fell I grabbed the tree limb with both hands. A loud crack sounded as the limb snapped off. In a split second, the lady in the navy blue suit reached up, caught me by the waist, and broke my fall. She lowered me to the ground with ease so I landed in balance on both feet, unharmed. Once again her strength and how she was able to hold my weight astonished me. She looked straight into my eyes with her reassuring smile, handed me a tissue to mop my face, kissed my cheek, and vanished.

"Wait," I called, "thank you — again." She was nowhere to be seen. I still held the tissue.

The school custodian came running. "That was an athletic landing!" he remarked. "I was really afraid you'd be badly hurt."

He was repairing a window shade, just happened to look out the upstairs window, saw the ladder fall, and came running to the playground as fast as he could. Asked if he saw another lady with me, he insisted I was alone.

I know she was there. Minutes after the incident, as before, I continued to feel her powerful grip. This had to be the school's guardian spirit again. These two incidents are the only times she rescued me. But sometimes I wonder if she guards the children and other visitors at that school. No one of her description was associated with the school in the past.

Only once, at a PTA meeting, did I hear another mother tell of being mysteriously saved from a fall on the inside stairs. I asked her about the incident, but she refused to talk about it. I hope someone else has experienced this wonderful protective spirit — she has exquisite taste in clothing.

Dr. Virginiae Blackmon is an author, photojournalist/traveler, lecturer, exhibiting artist, spinner, and weaver. She has published articles on botany and scanning electron microscopy for science journals, medical articles for reference books, and has written for regional newsletters and national magazines on spinning and weaving. Her expertise is in the fields of journalism (news reporting), photography (journalism and art), medicine, botany, general science, travel, and fiber arts.

Our Resident Ghost

Anne F. Skalitza

I stand at the curb, looking at my house that was built in the middle of the twentieth century. A well-kept white Cape Code with black shutters. Orange and yellow mums sit sentinel by the front door and a cheery welcome sign greets visitors. It is a sunny and well-maintained home, where the rooms open to each other. No hidden nooks or crannies or tucked-away staircases. No floor boards that creak, windows that rattle, or peeling paint on the walls. In fact, this house doesn't even have an attic, just a tiny crawl space above the bedrooms. The basement is dry and clean and well lit; no cobwebs there. As far as I know, no one has died in this house, and the land it sits on was a horse farm for as far back as anyone can remember. Nothing spooky or scary about *this* house, the home I have lived in for nineteen years.

Yet it harbors unexplained and totally unexpected happenings. I have read that ghosts can sometimes act like twelve-year-old boys, pulling pranks, making things go "bump" in the night, or wreaking havoc. Well, we have a ghost (and I believe it is just one spirit) that acts like a woman, a very young child, and yes, even a twelve-year-old boy.

When my second son was eight months old, and we had been living in this house for three years, strange things started happening. One night at around midnight, the baby woke up crying as if he were truly scared by something. My older son, always a deep sleeper, was in a bed near him, and didn't wake up.

I went to comfort the baby, and as I rubbed his back, there was a steady banging noise echoing throughout the downstairs. My heart skipped a beat as I went to get my husband and he, too, heard it and went down to investigate. The noise stopped as soon as all the lights were turned on. Our son immediately calmed down. A perfunctory look around the first floor showed that nothing was amiss. With a shrug of the shoulders and a kiss goodnight, we went back to bed. I lay under the covers, waiting for the sound to start up again, but after an hour of intently listening and nothing happening, I finally fell into a disquieted sleep.

The next morning I went downstairs and passed the children's neatly kept playroom. As I glanced into it, I saw my sons' wooden toy hammer lying on the wood floor, all by itself. All of the other toys were on the shelves where I had placed them the night before. I went into the room and picked up the hammer, lightly banging it on the floorboards. It resounded throughout the house, making a noise similar to what we had heard the previous night. I quickly replaced the hammer on the shelf where it belonged, a shiver running down my spine.

A few years later a friend of ours was staying overnight on the pullout couch in our den. He had just settled his head onto the pillow and closed his eyes when he felt a presence slowly climb onto the bed, and then across his legs and up along the side of his body, like a sensual woman would. His eyes flew open and he looked around. No one was there. The following morning, our normally skeptical friend sat at our dining room table, hands cradling his steaming cup of coffee as if it were a life preserver. His eyes stared straight ahead as he related the night's strange encounter. What happened to him was very real and more than a little nerve-racking.

One winter's evening several years after that, some friends, my husband, and I were watching television in the den. The sleigh bells that hang on the inside of the back door started ringing. The sound was clear and distinct, as if someone had picked them up and dropped them back down. We all went to that door but no one was there. And that night there was no wind. We even checked the door and it was locked.

The last episode took place a few years ago. It was three o'clock in the morning and I was lying in bed, staring at the ceiling, unable to sleep. Something was bothering me, and I couldn't place what it was. All of a sudden I heard soft child-like footsteps coming from the downstairs. Someone walked through the kitchen, picked up a bowl, and then put it down. A cabinet door was slowly opened and closed. I waited, not daring to move and holding my breath so that I could hear. The footsteps then continued to lightly pad through a few rooms down below and then silence. I knew it wasn't a burglar because all the windows and doors are always locked, and these footsteps were definitely a very young child's. My boys were now teenagers and made a lot of noise even when they try to be quiet. Just to be sure, though, I quietly got up from my bed and investigated. My sons were in their bedroom (which was on the second floor with us), and they were sound asleep. I didn't bother to go downstairs. By this time, I knew who it was, or rather who it wasn't.

It has been a while since we've heard anything out of the ordinary, but I know it's just a matter of time. Our resident "ghost" (or spirit or phenomenon) is a curious one, investigating, maybe trying to see if our home is a place it would like to stay. Permanently.

 Anne F. Skalitza is a freelance writer and published author of several essays and short stories in national magazines and online, such as *The Family Digest, Alive!*, Short Stuff For Grownups, and AlienSkinMag.com. She also has a novel for preteen and teenage girls, *Lost And Found Love*, published by Koenisha Publications. Anne is married to Joe Skalitza and has two teenage sons. She lives in New Jersey, three blocks from the Atlantic Ocean. Visit her web site at http://www.geocities.com/stormie267.

Visiting Grandma's House

Yolanda Falcon

My Grandma Carrie had a flair for spinning ghost tales. Yet she vowed they were all true accounts.

Grandma swore she saw apparitions at her home in Woodsboro, Texas. She said that they most often occurred when she was grieving over a deceased relative she missed. She believed souls weren't able to find peace as long as their family members continued to mourn them. According to Grandma, if they were out of mind, they'd stay out of sight. With that thought in mind, I would've bid a quick *adios* to those who'd passed away if I'd been her.

I always wondered whether Grandma could really see ghosts. I truly hope not, because that would be one trait I'd hate to inherit.

One of the most bizarre stories she told was about a handsome stranger who knocked on her screen door at sunset one hot summer evening. She said he was dressed to kill, in a three-piece gray pin-stripped suit and a fedora. He was tall, slender, and had a nicely trimmed mustache. The way she described him, it was obvious she had checked him out from head to...well, I can't really say toe, considering what she saw. When she lowered her gaze to the cuff of his pants, she expected to see a pair of well-polished shoes, but to her dismay, she said she saw what appeared to be a large pair of rooster feet. She said a chill penetrated the screen door as he tipped his hat, smiled at her, and vanished before her eyes.

Whatever it was that paid a visit to Grandma that evening, she maintained it had to be evil. I simply take it as a sign that no man is perfect.

Despite all the spooky encounters she claimed she had at her house, that's the only place she felt at ease. Grandma often said, "Being in a big city like Houston makes me nervous." I suppose Grandma didn't find "wandering spirits" as unnerving as one would think.

When Grandma made up her mind about something, there was no changing it. One time she came to Houston with the intention of spending a couple of months with us, when suddenly, after only a few days, she got homesick and insisted she be taken home that very night. My parents knew it was futile to try to persuade her to stay, so they packed the olive-green family Buick as soon as my father got off work. The 400-mile round trip would take at least nine hours, because of the countless bathroom stops Grandma always had to make along the way. She was a firm believer in the benefits of drinking water. Lots of water.

Since I was about thirteen years old at the time, I had no choice but to tag along on that impromptu trip. My parents sat in the front, while I had the privilege to sit in the backseat with Grandma and all of her excess baggage. In my opinion, the best way for her to have traveled was in a U-Haul.

By the time we arrived at my grandmother's house it was close to midnight. Even though she lived near the center of town, there wasn't a car in sight at that hour.

After all of Grandma's gear was unloaded, I decided to stretch out in the backseat of the car while my parents went inside and helped unpack her belongings. All the windows were rolled down and the light inside the car was on. Despite the notorious reputation my grandmother's place had for eerie sightings, I usually felt safe there, so I just laid my head on the pillow and basked in the comfort of having the entire seat to myself.

It was a balmy, moonless night. The crickets were in symphony. "This must be the peacefulness Grandma misses when she's away from here," I murmured.

The tranquility of the moment quickly faded when I heard someone lean against the hood of the car. Then came the sound of someone breathing deeply.

Knowing my father often suffered from shortness of breath due to a heart condition, I asked, "Daddy, are you okay?"

When no one responded, I figured my father was trying to scare me, considering the practical joker he was. For a laugh, he'd flip his eyelids back during horror movies just to frighten us. After a long pause, I noticed it sounded more like a woman breathing.

In a quivering voice, I said, "Daddy, if it's you, tell me now, because you're really scaring me."

Once again no one responded. By then, I knew it wasn't my father. The breathing got heavier as I heard it approach my side of the car. My skin began to crawl as I sensed a presence reaching in to grab me. I screamed. Seconds later, I heard my grandmother's screen door slam. My father came running to see what was the problem. After I told him what had happened, he said he hadn't seen anything around the car when he came out. In an effort to calm my fear, he tried to explain the incident away by saying it could've been a stray dog. Sure, it must've been a really tall dog, I thought.

Of course, Grandma had a totally different explanation. She said several people in town had told her they'd seen a faceless woman wearing a sheer white gown. She'd been seen at dusk, moving in a floating motion, her feet never touching the ground. My grandmother said the woman was believed to be a lost soul. If it happened to have been her near our car that night, I must've sent her bolting to her grave, the way I hollered.

I always thought my grandmother exaggerated when she said her property was inhabited by restless spirits. That was until I had my own personal encounter with the unknown.

Even after all these years, I'm still bewildered by Grandma's outlandish ghost tales.

Did I say tales?

Yolanda Falcon is a native Houstonian who graduated from the University of Houston with a BA in Psychology. She considers herself a "writer under construction." Her work has been published in the *Houston Chronicle*, *Suddenly IV, Suddenly V, Women's Journal*, and *Promise Magazine*. She also enjoys writing short plays and monologues.

Ghost House Out of Gladewater

Lucile Davis

Ghost stories usually conjure up thoughts of cold spots, unearthly noises, and see-through people. My story is a bit different. I experienced this brush with the paranormal at the age of twelve, so I usually credit it to an overactive imagination. The thing is my experience was shared by a dozen other twelve-year-olds girls on the way to lunch and a day of shopping in Dallas. Shopping doesn't usually create visions of the afterworld, does it? Who knows with twelve-year-olds?

This all happened back in the dark ages when train travel was still an option. My Camp Fire troop of Longview, Texas, decided its "dream" field trip would be a trip to Dallas to have lunch in a fancy restaurant, then go shopping at Neiman Marcus. Taking the train into the big city was the cheapest, fastest way to get there.

It was spring, so we expected our bright idea for a field trip to be met with a sunny day. Our plans made, permissions granted, and tickets purchased, we waited impatiently for the big day. It dawned dark and damp with a hint of chill in the air. The bad weather didn't dampen our enthusiasm for the trip though. Dressed in our Sunday best, hose, heels, and hats included, we gathered at the train station.

The stationmaster greeted us with news the train would be a bit late. Seems the water was up over the tracks between Lufkin and Longview. The delay turned down the energy level in the train station a bit, but not much. After an hour's wait, the echo of girlish chatter in the high-ceilinged station seemed to get louder by the minute. I was not a happy Camp Fire Girl. Endless gossip about Frankie Avalon or Elvis Presley bored me silly and my girdle was killing me. Yes, in those days we wore that particular instrument of torture.

Ten minutes later the train pulled into the station, putting a stop to the chatter. We clambered aboard and took seats on the station side of the train so we could wave to those on the platform. The day had gotten a lot darker and rain fell as if poured out of a huge bucket. The train crept out of the station. Two city blocks down the track the rain was so heavy we couldn't see the sign on the roof of the station that read "Longview."

An hour down the tracks the train was still creeping along. The thrill of the train ride was over, replaced by restlessness. A number of the girls were making trips to the dining car for Cokes. My head was stuck in a book. I remember thinking how quiet the car had become. I looked around and found I was by myself except for an old couple asleep at the other end of the car. Strange, I thought. The troop chaperones were usually very careful not to leave any of their charges alone, anywhere.

The train lurched. I heard, or felt, metal trying to grab metal. The whole train seemed to shudder, then the wheels of the car I rode in seemed to hit a bump and stopped.

"Huh!"

I turned around to find Mrs. Johnson, one of the troop chaperones, on the aisle floor. I hopped up to go help her up.

"What happened?" I asked her.

"I don't know. I was standing, then I wasn't," she replied.

That's when I felt it. The cold. Suddenly I was very cold. I shivered and the chaperone must have felt it too, because she said, "Why is it so cold all of a sudden?"

I'm big on logic, so I headed for the space between the train cars to see if the upper part of the door was open. Sure enough! It stood wide open, the rain and wind pouring in, making the metal floor wet and dangerous. I started to close the upper half of the door but stopped to focus on what lay just beyond. A huge, white plantation style house with columns and a veranda stood nestled in a dense forest of trees right next to the train. If the whole door had been open, I could have stepped out onto that wide, empty porch.

I blinked and looked again. The house, columns and all, was still there.

"That's a gorgeous house," Mrs. Johnson said. "I wonder who lives there?"

Thank goodness someone else sees it, I thought. But why am I skeptical, I wondered. Then I saw it. There was movement at the front windows. At first I thought the curtains were solid, then they seemed to be transparent sheers. Something moved behind the curtains. I looked from one window to the other and realized I wasn't seeing into the house, I was seeing through it to the trees. As if to confirm my findings, a strong blast of wind swept through the trees making them sway, trunks and all.

A choking sound made me turn back to Mrs. Johnson. Her face lacked color and she looked as if she'd seen a... well...

you know. The train began to move again. I refocused on the open door to watch the plantation house. For a few moments it looked like any building viewed from a moving train, then the lines of the building began to be less sharp, less defined, less visible. I blinked to clear my eyes of the rain. When I opened them again the building was gone. I turned to see if Mrs. Johnson had seen what I saw. She was gone also. I dashed into the passenger car. At first all I could see was the sleeping couple at the other end of the car.

As I moved down the aisle, I could see Mrs. Johnson slumped in her seat and holding her head. I didn't try to talk to her; I knew I wouldn't get a response.

Screeches and giggles behind me announced the arrival of the rest of my Camp Fire troop. They were full of talk about the big white house at the side of the tracks.

"Did you see it? Wasn't it wonderful?"

I didn't say I'd seen it; I just asked the others what they saw. I got ten versions of the same story. The other chaperones hadn't seen a thing. They were at a table on the other side of the dining car. The chaperone who'd been with me never said a word.

Years later, older and more skeptical, I've tried to find the spot. Never found it. All I'm sure of is the house appeared somewhere just outside of Gladewater. One old man, sitting outside an ancient gas station, 'fessed up to seeing it once.

"Was on m' way home," he said. "Rainin' like hell, it was. Took the Farm Road instead of the new one. M' ol' car choked on the high water and I had t' stop. I looked back and there it was. When the rain slacked up a mite I started the car. When I looked back to see if anyone was in the house, it was gone."

The train no longer runs from Longview up to Dallas, but if they ever renew the route you might take a rainy-day trip down those old tracks to look for the ghost house outside of Gladewater.

Lucile Davis is the author of eighteen children's nonfiction books and a feature writer for newspapers, magazines, and The Emporium Gazette, an e-zine for writers and artists.

She is also an instructor for the Institute of Children's Literature, an accredited correspondence school advertised through *Writer's Digest* and other sources.

Colorado

Amanda Nagy

I t all started when my family and I lived in Colorado.
My husband was the (Army) Staff Duty Officer that
night so he would be gone all night. My middle daughter, Brooke (a ninth-grader), and Stacie, my youngest daughter
(a fifth-grader), were watching TV in the family room downstairs. Stacie had a friend visiting. I was in the living room
reading and enjoying the peace and quiet with our dog, Lucy, at
my feet. As I recall, one of our cats was in the room as well
because I remember her reaction. She sat straight up, staring
intently at something, like she did when she was stalking
something

The stairs leading to the bedrooms are on the opposite
side of the room. I love to read and get pretty deep into whatever I'm reading, so I have no idea how long it was before I
realized that Lucy was growling very deep and softly and her
hair was standing on end. I then heard a creaking sound that
turned my blood to ice water in my veins. It was the kind of
sound a floor makes when you step or stand on a loose board in
the floor. It sounded as if someone was deliberately making the
noise and it went on for several seconds — creak and pause,
creak and pause. I now know what it means to freeze in place. I
could not have moved if my life had depended on it. My chair
was situated just far enough to the right of the stairs that I

couldn't see the hallway. I knew where the sound was coming from though. The floor outside of Stacie's room would creak every time you stepped on it. I finally worked up the courage to get out of my chair and walk over to the stairs. I was absolutely convinced that someone was in the house with us. It didn't occur to me until later to wonder why Lucy hadn't done more than growl. We had a prowler while living in Maryland once — again while my husband was gone (this time out of the country) — and she nearly tore the house apart trying to get to the would-be intruder.

I didn't see anyone standing in the hall, so I went into the kitchen and got a knife. I then went down to the family room and got Brooke and a cordless phone. I took her aside and told her what had happened and asked her to follow me with the phone while I checked the house. I told her to run away and dial 911 if we found anyone. We crept all over that house with the dog close beside us. I have not been that scared very many times in my life. I expected someone to jump out and grab me at any moment. We didn't find a thing, but it was just the beginning of many scary moments.

I have no idea why, but almost all of the incidents that followed this happened when my husband was gone. He spent a great deal of time at Fort Ord, California, while we were stationed at Fort Carson, Colorado, so he missed out on most of the "fun."

My husband's closet doors were mirrored bifold doors. One night as we prepared to go to bed, Lucy, whose bed was right next to those closet doors, stood and stared into the mirrors and growled soft and low. I begged her to please not do this! I opened the doors to check but didn't find anything out of place. She eventually settled down and there were no more problems that night, but I don't think I slept very soundly.

On another night, Stacie had a friend spending the night so they were sleeping on the sleeper sofa in the family room. It was around midnight when I heard the sound of someone running up the stairs. I figured one of the girls got scared and waited for whomever to come running in. I waited some more. No one came in, so I got up to check and found both girls sound asleep in the family room. I went downstairs to Brooke's room (she had a converted basement bedroom) and found her asleep as well. The dog was in her basket and the cats were curled up on the furniture. I doubted seriously that it could have been the cats anyway, since they weren't big enough to make that much noise. I went back to bed and just as I started to drift off, I heard someone run up the stairs again! This time I didn't wait and jumped up to see if I could catch someone in the act of trying to scare me, but of course no one was there. I went back to bed and when I heard it a third time, I decided to roll over and ignore it. Whoever or whatever it was lost interest when I ignored it so I had a peaceful rest of the night.

I do remember three incidents that took place while my husband was home. One was kind of funny, another nearly broke my heart, and the last one nearly scared me senseless.

We were all sitting in the family room watching a movie one evening when an M&M candy wrapper suddenly flipped through the air *out of nowhere*! No one had been eating, and in fact, we couldn't remember the last time anyone had had M&M's! We all kind of chuckled, but it was creepy at the same time.

The second occurrence happened while I was once again sound asleep. I woke from a deep sleep and couldn't figure out why for a few seconds. I lay there and listened, then realized I heard a very faint sound of a young child or toddler crying for Mommy. This was coming from the hallway outside our bedroom, which would be where my husband's closet extended into the wall. It broke my heart to hear this small voice crying and fortunately, it didn't last long. Was I dreaming? I don't think so. I believe I was wide-awake. My husband slept through it though, so I can't be certain. He didn't sleep through the last time.

Once again, deep in the night I heard crying. This time though, it was Stacie. She sounded absolutely terrified so I jumped from our bed and ran across the hall into her bedroom. Ernie woke up too, but being a mom I was quicker to jump and run. I found her on the floor struggling and screaming for help. She was prone to night terrors as a younger child, but hadn't had one in several years. When I got her to wake up a little bit, she told me a man had been trying to pull her "down the hole." Normally, I wouldn't have been terribly concerned, but in light of all the other scares, this one chilled me to the bone. It still does when I think about how terrified she sounded.

We did have one very funny incident, though at the time I was too mad to laugh about it and the kids knew better than to laugh. Brooke and Stacie were at the stage where they argued constantly, day and night, and they always managed to drag Mom into the fray, which absolutely drove me wild. Our family room was down a short flight of stairs, just off the kitchen. There was a smoke detector in the ceiling at the top of the stairs. They got into argument #19 of the day and as always, one of them called "MoOoOm!" I was in the kitchen and walked over to the head of the stairs in an absolute passionate fury. I was so *sick* of being dragged into their petty arguments!

I started to holler and carry on as only Mom can, when suddenly the smoke detector (which was right over my head) started beeping! We all look back now and laugh, but as I said, they knew better than to make a sound at the time. So, whatever, whoever it was had a sense of humor.

We only lived there for eighteen months, so I have no idea if things would have continued happening. We owned the house, and rented it after we left, but none of our renters ever reported any strange or scary moments. This may be because whatever it was followed us to Alabama — but that's another story.

Amanda Nagy and her husband, a career Army officer, retired from the military at the end of 1999. All of the events written about in "Colorado" and "Knock, Knock, Who's There?" took place during their years in service. Her passion for writing short stories began while in high school, but once she started a family the desire to write took a backseat. It has only been in recent years that she has again started writing. Everything she writes is "true-life," frequently about family and often humorous, since it involves the antics of her grandchildren and/or the dumb things she manages to do almost daily. She currently lives in North Carolina with her beloved husband. She is a stay-at-home nana and baby-sits her three grandchildren. In her spare time, in addition to writing, Amanda loves to read.

Old Man Tiller's Ghost

Riley Froh

Necessity prompted us to move into the old Tiller house in the 1950s. It was haunted, folks said, by the ghost of Old Man Tiller, and it was available because no one else wanted to live in it. Having just lost our home and land in a bad business deal, we were hard up for a roof over our heads and weren't too picky. The Tiller place seemed our best option. So we cut a deal with the heirs and moved in.

Under our circumstances, the story that Old Man Tiller prowled this dwelling in spirit form allegedly searching for his hidden money didn't trouble us in the least. But from the start we sensed that there was something different about our new home. You just never felt you were alone, even if you were certain you were. There was a sense of someone just having been there before you as you walked around from room to room. Yet, the sensation was not oppressive. Whatever it was — imagination or reality — the thing wasn't uncomfortable, and I speak from experience.

I had once had a disturbing encounter with the spirit world that was most uncomfortable. My boyhood friend, Richard Callihan, and I were the first hunters around Luling, Texas, to call up predators by making the sound of a dying rabbit. Coyotes, bobcats, and foxes responded to our mimicry and it was fascinating to watch these sly creatures slink out of the deep woods.

One gorgeous autumn day, what we called Indian summer, we crept into a promising thicket in territory new to us. We always sat quietly for some time before starting to call. But as the stillness settled in, an unseen pall enveloped us like a fog. The weight of a depressing thickness wreathed around us, oppressing us even though the air remained bright and clear with no visible change. Only in our senses did we know something was wrong.

I glanced at Richard, whose face mirrored my own unease. He cut his eyes back the way we had come. Without a word we stole away from the spot. Curiously, we never spoke of the matter. The experience was just too real and too disturbing to bring up again. Even when I found out that years before a lynching had taken place from a railroad trestle not far from where we sat, I could not bring myself to discuss the event. It was that eerie.

The presence in the Tiller house, however, had no such sinister overtones. There was a lightness and sense of humor about the place. If the specter did exist, it was a Casper the Friendly Ghost, not Banquo's bloody apparition haunting Macbeth or Jacob Marley's tortured spirit rattling his chains and disturbing Scrooge. If some poor spook needed to exercise his unrest in the rambling old house we were so happy to be in, we didn't care. After all, it once was his, and he became a family joke among us, giving us some laughs during hard times.

Then the familiarity became a little more personal. You could not keep the door to the den closed. You could rattle the catch and be sure it had caught, but it would slowly swing open at some point. We looked at it not as an annoyance but rather a game to be played with our phantom host. My mother was a great wit and was always ready with a clever pun about the mystery. "Old Man Tiller shouldn't worry. We don't have a ghost of a chance of finding his money," she once quipped. My stepfather, who possessed a more practical humor from the Luling Oil Field where laughter remedied the dangerous work, began to talk to the ghost.

"Hey, Old Man Tiller," he would yell, "keep that door closed!" We could sense Old Man Tiller laughing, even though he didn't make a sound. We all began to talk to the odd fellow, much as people talk to themselves or to their dog or cat when alone too much, not really expecting an answer but merely being sociable.

Old Man Tiller changed tactics. Now, when he moved from room to room, he creaked the floorboards a little. The sound effects were perfect, as though someone were taking slow, deliberate steps. He was best at this new haunting device in the quiet hours after midnight, when sounds were rare in our little town.

Perhaps he was disappointed in the lack of response because for the first time he started coming up the long flight of stairs to my room. I remember playing the game one night.

"Hey, Old Man Tiller," I challenged firmly. He stopped. But, after an appropriate rest to lull me back to sleep, he started creaking up again.

"Go back down, Old Man Tiller," I ordered firmly. He turned and cracked and creaked back down the steps, sadly, I imagined, to his happier haunts below.

So far, I was having a grand time with the ghost, even though I was uneasy with his presence on the second floor where there was no way of escape except the staircase. As someone who categorically denied the supernatural as a matter of philosophy, I sought out natural answers to explain away the phenomenon.

I talked to the local petroleum engineer, Ken Blackmar, who had mapped the Luling Oil Field. He had a simple answer as to why the house creaked and groaned. The Tiller home sat diagonally right on top of the fault line that ran through the town. This break, or fissure, in the Earth's crust is what sealed off the oil flow far below, trapping the black gold being pumped out all around the area. Recent drilling operations involving small explosions set off below the well to increase the oil flow had disturbed the surface ever so slightly. The movement in the early morning hours as the house settled over the uneven fault line with the change in nighttime temperatures brought about the cracking sounds in the joints of the old lumber. The antique door latches didn't catch well in the keepers so the door would simply come loose and swing open with gravity at times.

This seemed logical. Except that the footfalls were so regular and the game with the door was so personal as the ghost played his pranks on us. It was much easier to explain it away when you were safely out of the house and you didn't feel the presence during such occurrences. But we were content to be a guest of the ghost of Old Man Tiller in his home. It was a good place to live at the time.

And then the whole matter became a moot question, a curiosity to be remembered with fondness and related with a smile during polite conversation when discussions turned to the supernatural. Happily, our economic condition improved and we were able to lease a bigger and better house, but the sojourn in the Tiller house had been a pleasant experience, one we never forgot.

The subject would come up from time to time. My cousin Richard Edwards had often spent the night with us in the Tiller place when both his parents were working. My mother spoiled her five-year-old nephew and he liked to visit us. Years later when he was a grown man, he told me he didn't like staying in the house but that he couldn't exactly say why. He never said anything at the time since he had no choice. Still, he was uneasy in the place. You can't help wondering about the situation when you get new revelations about the past.

My good friend Texas artist Wendell Williamson told me a story out of the blue that caused me some reflection about the Tiller ghost. Wendell was hunting as a guest on a fine deer lease in West Texas. The rancher told the party they could stay in an old, empty ranch house if they wanted to but that it was haunted. Wendell is a devout Christian and he isn't afraid of the devil himself. He and his wife went inside and got into their bedroll in an interior room out of the cold air while the others all stayed outside.

I asked him what it was like in the haunted house. "It was interesting," he said. "There was a strange feeling in there that I can't explain, but I ignored that and went to sleep. Then the doors that we shut into the other rooms kept opening and closing off and on. Of course, we ignored that too and went back to sleep."

I knew well of what he spoke.

Riley Froh has recently retired to his hometown of Luling, Texas, to write full time after teaching Texas history, U.S. history, and British literature at San Jacinto College for twenty-eight years. Froh is descended from original settlers of the town and grew up hearing the legends and lore of Luling, such as the story of the haunted Tiller house.

He is married to Mary Binz of San Antonio, who is also retired from San Jacinto College, and she is his best critic and proofreader. They have two sons, William Travis Froh and Noble King Froh.

He has published two non-fiction books: *Wildcatter Extraordinary* and *Edgar B. Davis and Sequences in Business Capitalism.* His eight short stories have appeared in *Louis L'Amour Western Magazine, Concho River Review,* two Western Writers of America anthologies, and one Berkley anthology. He has written several non-fiction articles and book reviews for scholarly journals. He is presently writing *Texas Eccentrics,* which is scheduled for publication next year.

Knock, Knock Who's There?

Amanda Nagy

So, we moved to Alabama. None of us were very happy about this situation, but that is another story. We rented a house when we first got there because we didn't expect to be stationed any longer than we had been in Colorado, which was eighteen months. Ultimately, we lived in Alabama for over six years and eventually bought a house there.

The rental house was a split-level with a lower level garage with the laundry room located in the back. I hated that laundry room. We had been living there for about a month when I went down one evening to check on some clothes that I had in the dryer. We were taking the kids to Six Flags Over Georgia the next day and we all needed clean shorts. Something odd caught my attention and when I looked closer, I saw a small snake lying on the floor. I *flew* up the stairs, screaming at the top of my lungs. My brave husband ran down to the garage, grabbed a shovel, and finally killed the nasty little thing, which turned out to be a baby copperhead. Our neighbor said he'd never heard of anyone in the neighborhood having a snake in their garage before. I despised going down there even more for the entire four years we lived in that house. I don't know if that was the cause of all the weird things that happened in that house, but it was the beginning.

I became a stay-at-home mom when we moved there, and my days were fairly quiet. I was in the habit of cleaning in the morning and enjoying the afternoon by reading or doing needlework. One afternoon, I was sitting in the living room with the TV off, just chilling out. The dog was asleep on the floor, when suddenly she leaped to her feet, ran towards the door to the garage, and started barking like crazy. I jumped up with my heart pounding because we had both apparently heard the sound of one of the garage doors being slammed shut. I knew the kids weren't due home for almost two hours and my husband was at work. So I ran to the front porch to see if someone was messing around out front. There wasn't a person in sight. It thoroughly shook me up since I knew I hadn't imagined it. The dog was proof of that.

A couple of weeks later, I was once again sitting in the living room. Lucy was asleep as usual and our cats were lying on the floor. (One cat was a huge scaredy-cat and would run to hide in a cabinet every time the doorbell rang. One Thanksgiving she spent an entire day hiding there!) Suddenly, the cat was headed for the cabinet and Lucy was on her feet barking at the garage door. It sounded like someone walked up the stairs, then started rattling the doorknob!! I think my heart stopped beating for a second. Thank *God* I am an obsessive door locker. I make sure the doors are locked even when we're all home. Whoever or whatever wasn't able to get in. This time I quickly checked the backyard as well as the front yard. The backyard was fenced with chain link and the gates were locked, but someone could certainly have jumped the fence. However, there was no sign of anyone.

We had a couple more incidents of doorknob rattling, and none of them were ever funny.

Shortly after we moved to Alabama, I got roped into being a Girl Scout troop leader. I had twenty-one girls from third to sixth grades. We decided to have a special Christmas dinner and show for the parents. With so many girls, we had to break it into two nights. Brooke opted to stay home both nights since she was a teenager and liked staying home alone. The first night went without a hitch. But shortly into the second evening, Brooke, who had recently gotten her drivers license, came walking into the Girl Scout hut. Her face was white and she was shaken up, but had calmed down some before she got there. She said she had been sitting at the dining room table eating her dinner. The dog and one of the cats were sitting and begging for food as usual. Suddenly, all three of them heard someone whistling in the garage, then they heard "it" walk up the stairs and start rattling the doorknob again! The dog went crazy and the cat took off running. I don't know how or where Brooke found the courage to leave the house, but she grabbed the keys to her dad's pickup truck and drove herself across town to spend the rest of the evening with us. Her dinner was still on the table when we got home.

A friend gave me a house blessing prayer when I told her about all the strange goings-on. I don't recall if I ever did finish trying this, but the strange occurrences did stop shortly after. We will all always believe there was something wrong in that house. Especially in light of the fact that our healthy and much-loved Lucy died suddenly. Both of our cats and two guinea pigs died within a year of her death as well. We don't know what killed the pigs, but my big old tomcat got very ill and died quickly. The scaredy-cat developed breast cancer and died a few months later.

A lot of weird things happened in Colorado, but it was only in the house in Alabama that I felt sincerely threatened.

We have since moved from Alabama to North Carolina where life continues to be fairly uneventful, at least as far as spooky happenings. We all fervently pray this continues.

Amanda Nagy and her husband, a career Army officer, retired from the military at the end of 1999. All of the events written about in "Colorado" and "Knock, Knock, Who's There?" took place during their years in service. Her passion for writing short stories began while in high school, but once she started a family the desire to write took a backseat. It has only been in recent years that she has again started writing. Everything she writes is "true-life," frequently about family and often humorous, since it involves the antics of her grandchildren and/or the dumb things she manages to do almost daily. She currently lives in North Carolina with her beloved husband. She is a stay-at-home nana and baby-sits her three grandchildren. In her spare time, in addition to writing, Amanda loves to read.

Out on a Limb

Olyve Hallmark Abbott

This tale is not to be confused with the old movie *On Borrowed Time*. It merely makes you think about it. That fable concerned an aged man with magical powers that allowed him to hold death at bay, hiding in an apple tree.

In the first place, the tree in this paranormal tale is a crabapple tree, not the regular variety in the movie. Inasmuch as these trees range in height from ten to fifty feet, a ghost can move around in a lot of branches as well as eat a peck of crabapples. This little fruit is sour at first bite, so the latter might not happen, even for a ghost.

Our apple-tree-spirit is named Kathy, who was not crabby at all. As a matter of fact, she taught in a North Texas subscription school in the late 1890s. Parents paid a minimal fee per year for each child's schooling. That money went toward paying the teacher's salary. Kathy was a gentle young woman and a beloved teacher. The little not-red schoolhouse had one room in which Kathy taught children from the first through eighth grades. My Great-aunt Ellen was one of those first-grade pupils.

The children had seen two crabapple trees near their teacher's house so they knew her liking for them. Kathy loved the fragrant blossoms covering the branches in springtime.

She brought a few cuttings to school where the fragrance permeated the classroom.

When she later gathered the fruit, the tasty sweet preserves and jelly that came from her kitchen were judged the best in the community. During a county fair, a young man took a fancy to Kathy and bought all the preserves and jellies she had for sale in her booth. He courted her until she said "Yes" to his marriage proposal.

At a time when many couples were married in the courthouse or by a traveling preacher, Kathy and her sweetheart, James, said their vows in the small country church. The church, decorated with apple blossoms, seemed for all the world to mark the beginning of a long and happy life for the newlyweds.

Unfortunately, that did not come true. The couple had been married less than a year when an influenza epidemic took hold. Kathy helped the sick, working non-stop in preparing broth and other food to take to neighbors. She spent many hours caring for others and little time caring for herself. Kathy succumbed to the disease. The doctor did what he could, but the young wife could go on no longer. She rallied a while, then took a turn for the worse.

Her husband sat by her side throughout the night. He fell asleep holding her hand, only to awaken to find his bride had breathed her last. Her death devastated him and he swore never to remarry.

The entire community attended her services in a small cemetery next to the church. The gathering included Kathy's pupils. They knew they would never find another teacher as fine. How could they ever learn with anyone else? They wanted to do something in her memory. One of the older boys suggested they plant a crabapple tree next to her grave. James agreed and made arrangements. The pupils dug the hole and James planted the tree. Each one helped pat the soil around the base of its trunk.

It took time for the tree to grow large enough to produce fruit. James visited Kathy's grave every day, mentally measuring the growth of the crabapple tree. After a while, it grew thick with branches. Buds appeared in April and soon turned into snowy white blossoms. The fragrance wafted across the entire graveyard. After the first tree withered, James planted another, and when students grew up, they planted the next.

James has long since died, never having remarried. He was laid to rest next to his Kathy.

Aunt Ellen told me when James made his regular visits he could see a vision of her among the spring blossoms. He sometimes saw her sitting against the tree, a wisp of blonde hair blowing across her face. She appeared to him only when the tree was in bloom.

Of course, I wanted to see for myself. A family legend? Some would say so. My aunt, who never believed in ghosts, insisted she had seen Kathy's apparition on two different occasions. Such words coming from Aunt Ellen caused my curiosity to rise. I've held a vivid sense of the paranormal all my life, although not what I call strong psychic abilities.

I told no one I planned a visit to the graveyard. I didn't want anyone to make suggestions or turn my thoughts in any specific direction. The focus had to be all mine. I drove to the cemetery alone one late April many years ago. The little church no longer stood — nothing remained but a crumbling foundation. Remaining in the car for a half-hour, I gazed at the tree and its white covering. People say one needs to be in a receptive mood to see an apparition — that is, if one wants to see.

I exited my car and walked across the new sprigs of green grass toward the tidy grave. I kept telling myself Kathy would appear. When I arrived at the site and looked into the tree's shower of white blossoms, my breathing became labored and my pulse quickened. The limbs touched each other, but a light breeze began to blow, parting the smaller branches of blooms. Was it my imagination? It had to be an apparition of Kathy — haze at first, then an outline of a face and shoulders.

Without realizing it, I called her name. She didn't answer. The branches folded together, not to reopen while I was there. The breeze ceased and I stood in a simple and peaceful country graveyard, alone. Perhaps I saw an apparition and perhaps I didn't, but it seemed very real.

One thing is certain. James will never sit under that apple tree with anyone else but Kathy.

Olyve Hallmark Abbott is the author of *Ghosts in the Graveyard: Texas Cemetery Tales*. She is currently working on *Haunted Jails, Courthouses, and Other Haints*. She has studied opera with Dame Eva Turner of the Royal Academy and has enjoyed a career in musical comedy, opera, and on national television.

One Last Good-Bye

Diane Kolb

The bond between people and animals has been the subject of many stories; some true, some imagined. Some, like this story, defy the known world. I have no explanation. But what happened to me was most definitely true and very real. I have a witness. Unfortunately, she'll never be able to corroborate the story.

Jacob, my sweet old cat, had reached the age of twenty. He suffered several strokes that left him totally deaf and gave his walk a little shimmy. He was a member of my little household seven years before my first child was born, so we shared a particular relationship. He knew from a look or a nod what I wanted him to do and he always did it. He would sometimes sneak from shadow to shadow around the kitchen table when I wasn't looking, to snatch the last bit of food left in the dog's bowl. All I had to do was catch his eye and give him my best angry look and he would quickly give up the adventure and slink into the next room. I got to know what he was feeling just by looking into his eyes.

Those last few days of his life were the hardest for me. Jacob was so brave. He wouldn't give in to death even when his internal organs stopped functioning. I knew that some animals, feeling their death near, would run away and find a dark, quiet place to die alone. When Jacob wasn't lying in his usual place by the kitchen door I knew I would have to search for him. He wouldn't get very far in his frail condition. I found him at the bottom of an outside stairwell, half submerged in dirty water, and knew what I had to do.

On the seat of the car, Jacob lay wrapped in a towel, purring very quietly as I stroked him. Even in his deteriorating condition he tried to comfort me as we drove to the animal hospital. The vet took one look at Jacob and told me gently it was time to put him to sleep. As I handed him over to the nurse, his big golden eyes met mine for the last time and I kissed him goodbye. I squeezed my eyes shut, spilling tears down my cheeks. Jacob was taken into another room and I made my way out to my car and collapsed in sobs, clutching the steering wheel. I had never experienced so great a loss. He had been closer to me than any living thing. The great void in my life opened like a giant chasm.

I could hear the distant rumble of thunder as I started my car. The rain began not long after I arrived home. It was like weeping. Jacob liked to sit on the window sill trying to catch the drops of rain running down the windowpane. As I watched the raindrops making zigzag patterns on the glass, my own tears joined the procession and the ache in my chest intensified. I did my best to get through the remainder of the day, presenting a brave front to my family. It was no use. My grief was all-consuming and sleep offered no peace.

The next morning after breakfast, I got the dog's leash out to take Cindi, my little sheltie, for a walk. The rain had cleared off and the sun shone on a crisp new day. Trees, heavy with moisture, dripped onto my bare shoulders and that wonderful smell of rainwater and freshly mowed grass filled the air. The sidewalks were still wet, and we had to skirt the deeper puddles as we walked along.

There was a lovely, quiet back street near our house where I loved to walk. The trees touched hands above me and long stretches of backyards rippled down to the road like the swells of a great green sea. I needed quiet comfort that morning and steered the dog down the street.

As we walked along, it suddenly became icy cold. Breezes that were still only a moment before blew at us like the blast from an open freezer door. Cindi shook her head several times. I tried to calm my goose bumps and wrapped my arms around myself. Then Cindi saw something. She became alert and her ears stood straight up, the way dogs do when they see a squirrel or another dog. She began to strain at the leash.

I followed the direction of her gaze. Breath stopped short in my lungs. There in front of us, coming out from under a small bush, was Jacob. I knew it was him by his labored walk with the little shimmy and his thin gaunt body. Cindi pulled forward on the leash while I stood there unable to move.

When the cat got to the middle of the road, he turned and looked right into my eyes. The moment I saw those golden eyes, I felt a wave of comfort run right through me. It was as if he were telling me that everything was all right. The ache in my chest melted away as I stood there. I think I looked away for just a second to collect myself, and when I turned back again, Jacob was gone. I looked around and noticed that our footprints made outlines on the wet blacktop where we had walked, but Jacob's did not.

Cindi and I ran over to where Jacob had emerged from under the bush on the right side of the road. There was a large expanse of lawn to the left in the direction he had walked, but no sign of Jacob. Cindi sniffed around for a little while but there was nothing there. As we continued, I turned around every now and then, trying to make sense of what happened. It made me smile.

Later I described this experience to several people, and they all looked at me as if I had lost my mind. But I know what I saw, and I wasn't alone. There was another witness, my little sheltie, Cindi. But she'll never be able to tell what happened. I only wish she could. The bond between humans and animals is a mysterious thing and fills me with wonder.

For all their arguments to the contrary, no one will ever be able to convince me that Cindi and I didn't see Jacob that June morning. I still believe that somehow he knew what I was feeling and came back to say one last good-bye.

Diane Kolb is a retired children's librarian, storyteller, and accomplished musician. She is a frequent speaker at schools and organizations with her many puppets in programs designed to encourage children to write. Her publishing credits include articles in *Cats* magazine and *Senior Magazine* as well as co-authoring *125 Reproducible Bible Puzzles for Kids Ages 6-8*, (Standard Publishing, 2000). Her first young adult novel, *A Star to Guide Me: A Journey at Sea*, received a five-star rating on Amazon.com. Her newest middle grade historical fiction novel, *My Father is a Clown* (PublishAmerica), will be out later in 2003. Diane is an active member of the Society of Children's Book Writers & Illustrators. She resides in Melrose Park, Pennsylvania, with her husband of thirty-three years and a retired racing greyhound.

Summer of 1965

Sharon Styer

In the long summer of 1965, we kids were shooed out of the house early and only called back in for lunch and dinner. We played jump rope, kickball, and freeze tag on the sidewalks and backyards up and down the street. I lived in the middle of the block so I could hang with kids who lived at the top of the street or at the bottom. This summer I was at the top of the street with Bonnie, Betty, Debbie, and Pat. We were all thirteen, fourteen, or fifteen years old.

After lunch, when the heat was up, we'd meet at Bonnie's side driveway. A huge maple tree spanned the whole side yard so that it was private and quiet and cool. Here we played board games and talked about boys, the Beatles, and any kind of clothing style that came from England. We played so many games of Clue that we used up all the scoring pads that came with the game. We were probably the only kids in the world who ran through those scoring pads. We were a persistent, compatible group of girls with time on our hands.

Towards the middle of July, Bonnie came out with a Ouija board for us to try. Her mother, Norma, was into psychic phenomena. She had a standing tale of her dead mother-in-law appearing every once in a while in her home. I didn't believe her for a minute. But I liked Norma and was amused by her stories.

We started messing with the board, and the plastic triangle game piece (called the planchette) would sort of jerk its way towards a letter. We were asking these vast questions: "Who will I marry?" "Will I go to England?" "Does Billy like me?" When the wand would actually move towards a "Yes" or "No," someone would claim that the other was cheating.

"I felt you move the wand," one would blame the other.

Bonnie and I were the only steady ones. I vowed not to cheat and I never did. I always trusted that she never cheated either. The idea of contacting another realm was intriguing to me. Bonnie and I would concentrate and the wand would start to glide around the board, only to head suddenly towards a corner with nothing there and topple off.

Then one day, out of nowhere, Bonnie says, "Who's the spirit on the board?" The wand heads down the board to the alphabet and spells out a name. I don't remember the first spirit's name; it could have been simple, like Bob. But we now had a name and the questioning began.

"Are you here near us?"

"Yes." Now this was getting good and creepy.

"Are you standing or sitting?"

"Sitting."

"Are you young or old?"

"Old."

Until someone asked, "How did you die?" "When did you die?"

The wand began to spell out whole sentences. We needed paper and pens to keep track. A story began to unfold. We started again:

"Who's the spirit on the board?"

"Jamie and Chad."

"Where are you?"

"Lying in a ditch."

"Where's the ditch?"

"In England. We were just in a car accident. No one has found us yet."

"Oh, my God!" we screamed.

Two English boys were lying in a ditch dead — no one had found them yet. This is the stuff of dreams for fifteen-year-old girls in 1965 in Amherst, New York. We were hooked on the Ouija board. We never left it alone. Day after day we sat at the board and asked, "Who is the spirit on the board?" We got really fast with questions as the dead people told us their tales. We asked about our grandparents and uncles. We asked if they were happy. We asked if they ate. "Do you wear clothes?" "Where do you get your clothes?" "Do you hang out together?" "Do you miss being alive?"

In my mind the spirits were like old black and white photographs in which they could finally move around and turn to me and speak. The women, if they were older relatives, were in flowered dresses. The men were in white shirts and slacks. Some wore hats; some smoked. We began having favorite spirits that we could beckon to the board whenever we wanted them. I saw them hearing their name and excusing themselves from wherever they were and coming to our board. Sometimes it took a few minutes and the wand would wander aimlessly around the board and then abruptly would start spelling out words, which meant they had arrived.

When it was fall and too chilly to hang out by the tree, we moved inside to my bedroom. Four or five of us would crowd into my room with the door shut. Unlike Bonnie's mother, my mother was very uneasy about what we were doing in there.

By this time, we had multiple boards going. We found we could use a shot glass upside down and a cut-out paper alphabet.

We needed a second board because of a strange occurrence one day. The wand had started circling around the board. It started going really fast and out of control. This felt very weird. We left the board and waited awhile, but the same thing happened again. So we made another board and asked the spirit on that board what had happened. That spirit told us we had a demon on the board and we would need a friendly spirit to get it off. Bonnie beckoned her favorite uncle. He told us we had a bad spirit on the board and that he would kick him off. He was so casual that I thought maybe he just had to wander over and have a little talk with that demon. But thoughts of dealing with a bad spirit, especially in my bedroom, made me uncomfortable. We started getting the demon on the board more often.

The culminating moment was the poem we received from two young children who had died in a house fire. Gibberish happened on the board one day, and then simple words were spelled out. We got a feeling that these were young kids. They answered that they were five and eight years old. Their home had burned and they were lonely and unhappy. I had begun to feel cynical and daring towards the board and its spirits. I had begun asking for physical proof. I wanted things to be moved around in my room, or show a little leg and become even a trace visible. To these children I said, "Give something to us and we'll be your friends." They said they'd write us a poem and asked us for five minutes. So we came off the board and hung out for five minutes. When we got back on, a simple rhyming poem was spelled out. We wrote it down and sat there astounded. I felt so badly for these kids. I wanted to hold them.

I wanted to comfort them and make them feel better. I also wondered what the hell I was doing hanging around with all these dead people. I felt I was intruding on something I didn't understand. I felt I had reached an edge that I should back away from.

We stopped playing with the board. School was getting more complicated and boys more fascinating. I kept the shot glass upside down in my room. Once in a while my hand would rest on its edge and I'd imagine a little pull. But I have since avoided the board. I learned that there is a world or an energy outside of this one. I've heard the theory that sometimes the dead are uncomfortable with their death — too sudden or too something — and their spirits can wander. I believe that. But I no longer tamper in their world, knowing that some things are best left alone. What could I possibly do anyhow?

Sharon Styer grew up in Amherst, NY. She studied creative writing in Berkeley, California, at the University of Washington, and at Phoenix College. She currently resides in Alpharetta, Georgia where she is a member of the Roswell Writer's Group. This is her first published story.

Night of the Black Devil

Jim Gramon

It was a dark and stormy night (awww, come on, it really was). Up to that point, the day had been quite nice. But that would soon change.

I had spent the afternoon doing one of my favorite things — taking a drive into the rolling Texas Hill Country. My journey ended in the legendary magical town of Luckenbach. The evening had been passed in the company of my old friend Hondo Crouch, often referred to as the Clown Prince of Luckenbach. As is the custom in Luckenbach, we sat around the campfire, pickin', singin', and storytellin' 'til late.

The evening was wonderful, with Hondo telling some of his special brand of humorous stories. Around midnight I said my good-byes to Hondo and the others and headed back towards Austin. The warm air felt good blowing through the car windows. By that time of night the warmth from the hot day was combining with the occasional areas of cool air that pooled in the low spots where the road dipped into low creek beds and valleys.

Between Johnson City and Dripping Springs the weather began to change. Clouds gathered, then lowered 'til they nearly touched the ground. They hung suspended only a few feet above the roadway, dancing ahead of my lights, sometimes absorbing all the light, sometimes reflecting it all back upon me. Time to slow down and shift to low beams.

I hummed while driving slowly through the night. By the time I reached Oak Hill, on the south side of Austin, it was raining steadily. It was the kind of cold rain that starts falling several miles up, chilling as it plummets towards Earth, starting the evaporative cycle all over again.

The clouds and fog were now at ground level, and they blew back and forth across the roadway. Occasional streaks of lightning flashed across the patches of black sky that peeked down between the dark blowing clouds. Flashes danced across the landscape, reflecting off the wet roads.

I never understood folks who are scared by bad weather. To me it was always fun to watch Mother Nature put on her shows. And tonight it was turning into a wonderful light show, complete with sound effects worthy of any orchestra. The 3D surround-sound system was blasting out all the highs and lows, shaking the windows in my car.

Five miles from my home I had the first shiver. Was it the cold rain? The normally pitch-black country road was unrolling before me. The foreboding feel of the night continued. Even the moon, which had been visible briefly, refused to peek out. Only the storm clouds, filled with driving rain and lightning, were apparent. The shivers came more frequently the farther I drove.

Soon, I was turning onto Slaughter Lane, a Farm-to-Market road. For those of you unfamiliar with country roads in Texas, these are lane-and-a-half wide blacktop roads so narrow that there is no middle stripe. Often at low-water bridges only one car could pass at a time. If you drove too fast, it was easy to find yourself piled up in the ditch, or a creek, after unsuccessfully trying to clear an oncoming truck.

But this was one of the "good" roads to my home. Much of the driving in the area at that time was done on gravel roads.

Numerous creeks crisscross the area around my home. A mile down the road, Onion and Bear Creeks merge in one of the most idyllic of settings.

But this night dealt with the ominously named creek that runs a mere hundred yards behind my home. The beauty of the stream, still pools, plants, and critters was undeniable. Yet one dark cloud hung over this pastoral scene. There were many stories about how Slaughter Creek had gotten its name.

Some of the stories centered around Indian raids against the settlers along the creek. Other stories involved Civil War battles from a hundred years before. More contemporary tales dealt with stories of the creek running red for days with the blood of livestock that area residents had slaughtered on the creek banks. There were even tales of families being murdered by unknown predators in their sleep, and thus the name.

But none of this was on my mind as I turned off of Slaughter Lane and onto Manchaca Road. My concern was watching the road ahead carefully, because I knew visibility was going to get worse as I descended down the small hill towards the low-water bridge that crossed Slaughter Creek. The fog had become one of those that eat your headlight beams, leaving you unable to see much beyond the hood of your car.

Faint headlights up ahead told me I wasn't the only person having to deal with this soupy weather. The oncoming headlights were now about a hundred yards away and barely visible. I slowed to allow the oncoming car to cross the narrow bridge first. When its headlights bounced upwards I knew it was across.

Closer and closer we moved towards each other through the thick fog, when a black shadow crossed between our headlights. At first I thought it was a reflection. But then I realized that this "reflection" had stopped in the middle of the road. There it was, blocking the headlights of the oncoming car, but only partially blocking the light. Some of the light seemed to pass through this black figure.

It was a horse! A beautiful black horse with a glistening coat. It turned and stared calmly at me, while I tried to bring the car to a safe stop. I've been around horses all my life. Know their moods and attitudes. What particularly concerned me was that there was no fear or nervousness in this horse's demeanor. Which was very unusual for one standing in the middle of a road with two cars bearing down on it.

I swerved to the right as the black horse calmly turned to face the other vehicle. That car also swerved towards the shoulder of the road.

Stray pieces of gravel crunched as the tires grasped for traction on the wet roadway. It seemed like forever before the cars came to grinding, crunching stops. Now, in this part of the country, stray animals on the roads were not a rare event. Old fences often led to roaming livestock. So I figured I would get out and herd the critter back towards home.

But it didn't happen that way this night. The horse continued to face the other car. And I was checking out the horse's backside, looking for a brand.

Then, without a hint of movement, this beautiful black horse just simply disappeared, even as the echoes of its hooves on the roadway died.

"What the hell?" came from the car in the opposite ditch. Then out came the perplexed face of my old friend, the sheriff. "Where did it go Jim?"

I didn't respond. Just shook my head. We both knew we had seen something unexplainable, yet neither of us was sure just what that was. The creature was gone, leaving the two of us shivering in the cold rain on the road by Slaughter Creek.

But the story didn't end there. As it turns out, this may have been just another chapter in a centuries-old story. Later I told the story to Hondo. He sat quietly, rubbing his stubble-covered chin.

"Jim, ever hear of Diablo Negro, the Black Devil?"

"Nope."

"J. Frank Dobie wrote about him. Seems he is a wild mustang that has roamed the central Texas area for hundreds of years. Dobie wrote about him in one of his books. Check it out."

I did check it out, and so can you, in J. Frank Dobie's book, *The Mustangs*. There you can read more about the legendary Black Devil mustang.

But always remember, there are many things in this world that we don't understand yet. So drive slowly on those foggy, rainy nights because some of those unexplained things may be standing in the middle of the road in front of you!

Would believe the biography of a genuine Texas storyteller? Probably not! In spite of that (or perhaps because of it), Jim hosts the annual Liar's Contests in Austin and Dallas. He grew up listening to storytelling legends like **John Henry Faulk** and **Ben King Green** at the Liars' Table in Cumby, Texas. In junior high he started writing music and singing with friends like **Roy Orbison**, **Janis Joplin**, **Willie Nelson**, **Steven Fromholz**, **Kinky Friedman**, **Allen Wayne Damron** and **Rusty Weir** during the birth of the "Austin Sound." He has had several short stories, poems and songs published, in addition to his three uniquely Texas books: *Famous Texas Folklorists and Their Stories* (Republic of Texas Press, 11/2000), *FUN Texas Festivals & Events* (Republic of Texas Press, 10/2001) and *Legendary Texas Storytellers* (Republic of Texas Press, 10/2002). Jim lives in scenic downtown San Leanna, Texas. He can be reached at Jim@JimGramon.com.

When Fear Turned to Pity

Tanya Sepulveda

Some people openly dismiss our stories as the superstitious ramblings of a bunch of crazy Mexican ladies, a bunch of wannabe *curanderas* who like a good story every now and again. But the women in my family know otherwise, for it is only the women who can feel the dead. It's a "gift" I never wanted much to do with really, but despite my best efforts, they keep coming back.

As far as I can remember, mother never told me about this "special ability" before my first experience with it. I was only a little girl after all, and I'm sure she didn't want to scare me. More importantly, I think she preferred to wait and see if I felt anything on my own. She didn't have to wait long. When I was six years old, I told my mother that my aunt, only a teenager at the time, was going to die. Without responding, I could tell she knew. The next day it happened. She told me years later that she had the same dream of my aunt's death, but prayed for a mistake in our visions.

Similar things continued to happen as I grew older. Until my early twenties, not a year of my life passed that a friend or relative did not die, and I was doomed to confront these people beyond their physical death. Perhaps because I myself was a child, however, it was only the young people who appeared to me. Never did my grandfather's siblings or older relatives make their presence known. This may be because they were old, sick, and content to die after a long life. But the young people were all victim to sudden tragedy, cut off from all potential promise. I feel this is why they came. They weren't ready to pass on and didn't quite know what to make of their own death, especially David.

Take every cliché of tragic deaths, and you have David's end. This is no disrespect towards him. On the contrary. His life was beautiful, full of meaning, love, hope, fun, friends, girls, and youth. I only say it's a cliché because this is what everyone says when young people die, but David's life truly encompassed all of these things. Everyone wanted to be his friend, every girl wanted to be his girlfriend. He and his siblings were perfect physical specimens, and all had personalities and intelligence to match. I was over the moon when David and I had that sort of quasi-courtship that only kids too young to drive, and therefore date, could have. It evolved into close friendship, for which I am thankful. Though I will always miss him, I doubt I could have handled losing a first love to tragic ends.

Though I know his death was an accident, I still don't know all the details. I never really felt I had to. My friend was gone, and that was all that ever mattered. I know he went into the hospital for minor surgery and should have been able to go home that same day. He even had plans with some of my friends to hang out that night. But something happened in surgery that was a freak accident and left him brain dead. Rumors circulated, clearly fabricated out of a series of miscommunications and mystery. But I listened without comment because I knew people were just trying to understand why someone so young and beautiful could die.

David survived on machines for a few days, and the halls and waiting rooms were literally filled with hundreds of friends and family around the clock. Especially given the hospital's responsibility for his death, they didn't turn us out. I'm sure it was a hazard to have us all there, but the volume of love for this person seemed unprecedented and they couldn't deny us these final moments. When he died, his brother, who was in the process of becoming a priest, led the rosary. Though such services are Catholic, the church was filled with people of all faiths. The walls of this enormous church were lined out the door, and the procession to the grave site took two hours. And though I know that David appreciated the love, these services are really for the mourners, not the departed. I know because he came to me a few years later filled with sorrow.

Usually, I saw my friends once or twice shortly after they died. They would come to me and stare with a startled expression, as if surprised by their sudden deaths and looking to me for answers. After a few seconds, their ethereal presence would vanish. David was different. A few times over the next couple of years, I swear I saw him out and about, and nearly forgot myself a few times as I began to greet him. But he always disappeared just as I stopped myself. I was convinced I was just imagining things because these sightings seemed of flesh and blood, not spiritual, as was usually the case when I saw a departed friend. Moreover, they occurred over the next few years. But after the events of a haunting summer night, I know that he was following me and his other loved ones. I was simply the only one who could see him back.

It was a typical night, and the only thing on my mind as I fell asleep was how much I enjoyed the book I had just finished, a fun new release by one of my favorite Latina authors.

Nothing I saw, read, or did that day prepared me for my one and only dream of David. I was in a hearse that was to be used to transport his casket to a new location. I don't know why this move was necessary, but dreams are often befuddling. As we were riding, David opened the casket and sat up. He was still in his burial suit and looked pretty much as we last saw him, save for a few sores and what looked like bruises. I awoke immediately from this dream with sheer horror. I sat up in bed shaking my head, crying in denial of what I dreamt. My room was still dark while I sat there. As I lifted my head from my hands, I saw him. I rubbed my eyes to make this vision vanish, but he stayed. He stood in the middle of my room pointing at his sores and bruises, and he spoke to me without moving his mouth. He clearly said, "Tanya, I'm so sad. I see all of you moving on with your lives, and I'm just laying in the ground rotting. Look at these marks. I'm literally rotting away, and I'm just so sad." And then he was gone.

My fear melted into pity. I have never before or since felt such sorrow. He never came to me again, and I fear that my sadness drove him further into solitude. My hope is that he was able to refocus his energy on his sister, a sweet young girl in her early twenties who has been fighting cancer for the last couple of years. If David has not found his way into the glorious afterlife he deserves, I dream that perhaps his sister is currently winning her battle because he helps her to live, having found a purpose in his death.

Tanya Sepulveda was born and raised in Corpus Christi, Texas. She graduated with a degree in Art History from the University of Texas in Austin, where she is currently working on a master's in Library and Information Science. After teaching middle school art for two years, she decided to dedicate some time to writing and illustrating, joining the Society of Children's Book Writers & Illustrators. This is her first published piece.

Ghosts, death, and anything macabre have always been a part of Tanya's life, having grown up immersed in a Mexican culture rich with eerie tales and practices. She respects the opinions of skeptics, but her experiences (many of which were simultaneously experienced by her mother) validate her belief in ghosts and premonitions.

Look For These Upcoming Books In The *Haunted Encounters* Series

Real-Life Stories of Departed Family & Friends

Real-Life Stories of Childhood Memories

Real-Life Stories of Haunted Houses

Real-Life Stories of Departed Pets

Real-Life Stories by Paranormal Investigators

Real-Life Stories by Ghost Tour Guides

Real-Life Stories From Around the World

Real-Life Stories from Travelers

And more to come!

Haunted Encounters
Writer's Guidlines

We'd love to read about your personal haunted encounter. Before sending a submission please read the following basic guidelines, and check our web site for the complete guidelines:

To be considered for publication, a submission should be based on a true, supernatural encounter that you have personally experienced.

Length requirements are somewhat flexible, but stories should be 1000-2000 words. Longer stories will be considered. Submissions under 1000 words will not be accepted.

Haunted Encounters is a series of books, each with a different theme. A submission that is not selected for one volume may be very appropriate for another.

Atriad Press
www.AtriadPress.com
P.O. Box 600745
Dallas, TX 75360-0745

We'll send you a *free* book**

Send us the name of your favorite independent bookseller and if they order 3 or more books from us we'll send you a thank you gift of a free copy of Haunted Encounters. We'd also appreciate your suggestions or comments. Use the form below, or contact us at our web site.

Atriad Press
www.AtriadPress.com
P.O. Box 600745
Dallas, TX 75360-0745
Attn: Editors

Here's the name of my favorite independent bookseller:

Store Name*_____

Address_____

City_____ State_____ Zip_____

Contact Person_____Phone/e-mail_____

Send my FREE book to:

Name_____

Address_____

City_____State_____ Zip_____

E-mail_____

Comments: _____

_____

_____

Thank you for sharing the adventure with us!
Ginnie, Dorothy, and Mitchel

* This offer not valid for stores associated or affiliated with any national bookstore chain.

** Store must order 3 or more books to validate offer. First postmark wins.